Dr. Khawaja Azimuddin is a gastro-intestinal surgeon in Houston, TX. He specializes in minimally invasive robotic surgery for colon cancer. He is a Fellow of the American College of Surgeons, the American Society of Colon and Rectal Surgeons, and the Royal College of Surgeons of England and Edinburgh. Though he has authored numerous scientific research articles, medical book chapters, and a surgical reference book, this is his first non-scientific work. In his free time, Dr. Azimuddin is an avid ceramic tile artist, and many of his large-scale murals are installed in public places. He uses his passion for arts to help build bridges between communities.

This book is dedicated to refugees all around the world.

Khawaja Azimuddin, MD

BOY REFUGEE

A Memoir from a Long-Forgotten War

AUSTIN MACAULEY PUBLISHERS
LONDON * CAMBRIDGE * NEW YORK * SHARJAH

Copyright © Khawaja Azimuddin, MD 2025

All rights reserved. No part of this publication may be reproduced, distributed, or transmitted in any form or by any means, including photocopying, recording, or other electronic or mechanical methods, without the prior written permission of the publisher, except in the case of brief quotations embodied in critical reviews and certain other non-commercial uses permitted by copyright law. For permission requests, write to the publisher.

Any person who commits any unauthorized act in relation to this publication may be liable to criminal prosecution and civil claims for damages.

All of the events in this memoir are true to the best of the author's memory. The views expressed in this memoir are solely those of the author.

Ordering Information
Quantity sales: Special discounts are available on quantity purchases by corporations, associations, and others. For details, contact the publisher at the address below.

Publisher's Cataloging-in-Publication data
Azimuddin, MD, Khawaja
Boy Refugee

ISBN 9798895433430 (Paperback)
ISBN 9798895433447 (Hardback)
ISBN 9798895433454 (ePub e-book)

Library of Congress Control Number: 2024923132

www.austinmacauley.com/us

First Published 2025
Austin Macauley Publishers LLC
40 Wall Street, 33rd Floor, Suite 3302
New York, NY 10005
USA

mail-usa@austinmacauley.com
+1 (646) 5125767

A special note of abounding gratitude to my parents, Mr. Khawaja Qumaruddin and Mrs. Fatima Qureshy Qumaruddin.

Table of Contents

Author's Note	11
Prologue	14
1: Trouble in the Land of Lazy Rivers	17
2: Adamjee Nagar	23
3: Amar Shonar Bangla	40
4: Ides of March	45
5: The War	51
6: The Fall of Dacca	56
7: A Narrow Escape	64
8: Back at the Cantonment	67
9: Refugees in Our Own Homeland	71
10: The Long Journey Begins	79
11: A Never-Ending Train Ride	85
12: POW Cage #1, Camp #34	91
13: Colonel Harnam Singh	96
14: Settling into Our New Life	100
15: Living in Oblivion	107
16: Prisoner of War Camps in India	114
17: A Kid's Wonderful World	119
18: Eat, Play, Pray, Sleep	125

19: Life Goes On	131
20: The Long Days	139
21: Terrible Times	144
22: The World Outside Camp #34	150
23: The News Everyone Was Waiting For	157
24: The Preparations	162
25: Return	168
26: After the End	171
27: Epilogue	175
Glossary	178
Reviews	182

Author's Note

The idea of writing a book about my childhood experience as a refugee and then a prisoner of war first came to me when my son began writing his undergraduate thesis about the 1971 Bangladesh Genocide. I grew up in East Pakistan and lived there until the Indo-Pakistani War of 1971, which resulted in the creation of Bangladesh. I was witness to both the war and its aftermath. After the defeat of our Pakistani Army and the surrender of Dacca, my family was taken as civilian prisoners of war by the Indian Army, and I spent the next two years in a POW camp in India. As my son interviewed me about my first-hand experiences, these painful memories came so alive that I started writing my own experiences that I present here in this book. So, first and foremost, I must thank my son Ahad Azimuddin for inspiring me to tell my story.

After I was released from the POW camp, I spent my teenage years in Karachi, Pakistan, where, with my mother's help, I fortunately wrote down some notes about our camp life. I have kept those notes all these years in my study, safe inside the little green suitcase that I carried with me on the day of my release.

Picture 01: My little green suitcase.

Almost fifty years later, these notes came in very handy for completing my memoirs.

I want to thank my brother, Khawaja Nizamuddin, and my sister, Nafisa Tahera, for their contributions to this book, especially my brother, who spent a considerable amount of time correcting and proofreading the manuscript. They were older than me, and their recollections helped me complete this book.

I am grateful to my wife, Sama, for letting me take precious time away from her to pursue my passions, whether for ceramic art, surgery, or writing. Finally, I am thankful to my daughter, Anam, and her husband, Samir, for making my life complete.

I am also grateful to my friends Salahuddin Ayubi, Naeem Ahad, Arif Iqbal, Ras Siddiqui, Fasih Soherwardy, Tarique Alam, Aamir Syed, Naeem Ahmed, and Syed Ali, who, like me, were all young boys caught in the unfortunate events surrounding the 1971 war. They went through their own harrowing experiences – ones no child should ever have to suffer. I am thankful to them for sharing their stories, some of which have been used here. Mr. Tarique Alam provided me with valuable information about some of the main characters of the camp and also provided me with two rare photos of the camp. To my knowledge, these are the only two pictures of the inside of the POW camps in India after the 1971 war, and I am excited to present these in the second edition of this book.

While researching for this book, I connected with Dr. Moin Bhatti, who is a psychiatrist in California and whose late father, Maj. Iftikhar-ud-Din Ahmad, was a military POW and wrote about his personal experiences as a Pakistani soldier in the book *Memories of a Lacerated Heart (1971): A War Memoir (From East Pakistan to Bangladesh)*. Dr. Moin Bhatti, who translated this book into English, has provided me with valuable insight into the events surrounding his father's war experience. Another veteran of the war is Colonel (Retd.) Nazir Ahmed, who wrote about the war in his book, *East Pakistan 1971: Distortion and Lies*. I was able to speak with him extensively about his recollections of the 1971 war and its aftermath. I am also thankful to Colonel (Retd.) Raj Bhalla of the Indian Army, who fought the battle from the other side and provided me with the Indian perspective on the 1971 Indo-Pakistani War.

I was fortunate to reconnect with Mr. Abul Quddus Nagi, who was the young and energetic cage commander of our POW group during the two years of imprisonment. I traveled to the small town of Cobourg, Canada, to personally meet him and obtain first-hand knowledge about life in our camp. Mr. Quddus had a thorough knowledge of everything that transpired in the camp since he was the civilian in charge of all the prisoners. While in Canada, I also hooked up with Mr. Shaukat Ali and his wife, Akhtar Sultana Ali, who were fellow prisoners, and he had played an important part in the day-to-day life of our camp. I am grateful to these friends for providing me with deeper insight into the events surrounding the Indo-Pakistani War of 1971 and our two-year confinement.

Above all, I am indebted to my parents, Mr. Khawaja Qumaruddin and Mrs. Fatima Qureshy Qumaruddin, who protected their three children and kept us from harm during those troubled times. They had the foresight to escape to the Dacca cantonment and stay with the Pakistani Army so that we were evacuated out of Bangladesh. They supported and nurtured us when we needed them most. They instilled in us our love of education and hard work and inspired me to be what I am today. Without their courage, I would have been lost, like so many others.

I would like to dedicate this book to all the refugees around the world. I sincerely pray that you find a new home where you are welcomed and are able to pursue your dreams and aspirations. You have faced hardships few can endure, and your experiences have made you strong and resilient. Now, you are ready to face the world and make your mark. Through hard work, dedication, and education, you will find that there is light at the end of the tunnel and that the future is bright and promising for you and your children.

Prologue

The Boy Refugee: A Memoir from a Long-Forgotten War is the story of my childhood caught in the Indo-Pakistani War of 1971. It is the story of my parents' resolve to escape certain doom, our two-year imprisonment in India, our day-to-day life in a POW camp, and our eventual repatriation to Pakistan. It is a story of chaos, oppression, atrocities, revenge, despair, and adversity. But it is also a story of compassion, as shown by the enemy who saved us, protected us, and provided for us for two years. It is a story of human resilience and of strangers coming together. Above all, it is a story of hope.

The 1971 war between India and Pakistan is a unique event. History has no parallel, in which almost a hundred thousand prisoners of war were interned in camps for two years and then transported a thousand miles across land to be returned to their country. I have attempted to bring this unusual story to the readers.

The Indo-Pakistani War of 1971 resulted in both the independence of Bangladesh and the dismemberment of a united Pakistan. For the Bengalis, it was an occasion for great jubilation and celebration, but to Pakistan, it was a great loss and a sad chapter in the country's history. Both sides paid a heavy price for this war. In war, there are no winners, and each side pays dearly with the lives of their loved ones; a victory for one side is a defeat for another. Most of all, each side looks at events from their own perspective. I chose to report the events as I saw them, from the eyes of an eight-to-ten-year-old Pakistani boy who got caught in the conflict. Others may remember differently. I must confess this is my story, and I apologize to the readers if my recollection of events is not what you expected.

Millions of people on both sides were displaced before, during, and after the 1971 war. The plight of these refugees is a sad chapter of history and a horrible reminder of the vagaries of war. Even today, nearly half a century later, many of those displaced during this war are still confined in refugee camps. For them, there is no resolution in sight, and the fate of these stateless people remains uncertain.

The 1971 Bangladesh Genocide is one of the least documented genocides in history, and that is why this story must be told. An unusual peculiarity of this genocide is that both sides committed atrocities, and large numbers of both Bengalis and Biharis were displaced and killed. In the years preceding the war, the Pakistani Army committed mass atrocities, and later, the Bengalis committed further atrocities in retaliation. I have attempted to bring to life the parallel perspectives surrounding the war and hope that it will interest both serious students of history as well as the casual reader.

While little has been written about the 1971 genocide, even less has been told about the fate of ninety-three thousand POWs in the aftermath of the 1971 war. This was the largest number of POWs taken during any war in history, with the exception of World War II. So, it is surprising that not much has been written about the lives of these prisoners. My story chronicles their day-to-day life in the internment camp. To my knowledge, this is the first book detailing the life of Pakistani POWs in the Indian camps.

I have set out to tell the story of my childhood in captivity because I believe it is as relevant today as it was fifty years ago. The world still struggles with the same problems and faces similar humanitarian crises, from mass migration, displacement, and forced relocation. Maybe we can learn something from our past.

The past few years have seen a renewed interest in the 1971 Indo-Pak War. The recent war crime trials in Bangladesh, the rise of ethnically motivated violence, as well as growing hostilities between India and Pakistan make this war relevant even today. As do the Muslim travel ban, the Central American refugee caravan, and stricter regulations for refugees entering the United States. More recently, the war in Ukraine and the tragedy in Gaza further underscore the catastrophic consequences of war and displacement.

The current refugee crisis has once again highlighted the plight of those forced to leave their homes under threat of persecution. Hundreds of thousands of refugees have entered Europe from war-torn Syria, Sudan, Burma, Somalia, Iraq, and Afghanistan. European countries do not have the resources to accommodate such a large number of migrants, and those refugees trapped in camps in Europe have no clear way out. I hope my book will bring more awareness to the refugee crisis and will be a stimulus for us to avoid making the same mistakes again.

On a personal note, I am a practicing colon and rectal surgeon in Houston, Texas. After resettlement in Pakistan and then in America, I have found that my dreams and aspirations came true. I pray that others will find happiness as I have. I have been in private practice in Houston since 2005 and specialize in the treatment of diseases of the colon, rectum, and anus. I have an interest in minimally invasive surgery and am one of the first surgeons in the United States to specialize in minimally invasive robotic surgery of the colon. I am a Fellow of the American College of Surgeons, the American Board of Colon and Rectal Surgery, and the Royal Colleges of England and Edinburgh. Though I have authored many scientific research articles and book chapters and have edited a surgical reference book, this is my first attempt at writing a non-scientific book. I hope you will enjoy it.

A portion of the sales from this book will be donated to the UNHCR.

1
Trouble in the Land of Lazy Rivers

Tears welled in Abdul's eyes as he embraced my father. He turned to my mother but could not bear to meet her gaze.

"Bibi Ji, I am sorry…I must go," Abdul choked as he murmured in his thick Bengali accent. He had summed up all the strength from the deep recesses of his frail body to utter those few agonizing words.

Ammi stood dumbstruck, silent, and motionless, but the sinking expression written all over her face was unmistakable. "You should leave now! We will be all right."

Abdul lovingly caressed my hair. He then kissed my sister, my brother, and me on our foreheads and said a final goodbye. He quickly tied his meager possessions into a bindle at the end of his staff, balanced the staff on his shoulder, and hurriedly walked out of our house.

I could not understand why Abdul, our long-time domestic worker, who had been a part of our household since before I was born, had to leave so abruptly. Pappa explained that Abdul had little children back in the village, and with all the unrest in East Pakistan, he needed to return immediately to his family's side so he could take care of them.

"But this was exactly what our Bengali security guard, 'Little Abdul', had said a few days ago when he, too, abruptly had to leave." My young mind was trying hard to comprehend.

I supposed that during times of trouble all men must go home to be close to their families. Perhaps that was why Pappa had stayed home from work for these last two weeks. I enjoyed having him at home. My school was also closed, so we all stayed home, the whole family together.

Picture 02: Family in 1968

I was eight years old and the youngest of three. My world consisted of little more than my daily trips to school, hanging out with my Bengali friends, and playing with my pet chickens and pigeons. We lived in a big house in Adamjee Nagar on the outskirts of Dacca, the same home where I was born and raised. There was a large pond behind our house, and tall coconut trees lined the other side of the pond. I would catch minnows with my fishing net basket and count the coconuts floating lazily across the water. To me, life was easy and fun.

Picture 03: Author in August 1964

Pappa had come to Adamjee Nagar in 1957, one of millions of Muslims who migrated to Pakistan after the partition of India in 1947 in search of a better life. During Partition, Pappa was a young college student in India, and after graduating, he immigrated to East Pakistan, where he found a job in the massive Adamjee Jute Mills complex. Over the next few years, he worked his way up to become a manager in Mill #3.

At the time, Adamjee was the largest jute mill plant in the world. It was located just a few miles outside the capital city of Dacca, in what was, then, the Eastern province of Pakistan. Thousands of employees worked around the clock in the mills to produce yarn, fabric, and sacking bags that were transported over the slow-moving tributaries of the Bay of Bengal Delta and then exported all over the world by ships.

But in those last few weeks before the Abduls left, the mills had been closed due to unrest and strife. During recent labor strikes, the Pakistan Army had slaughtered many mill workers, and then, in retaliation, the Mukti Bahini Bengali resistance movement killed many Pakistani military officers and civilians. Thousands of innocent people on both sides were killed. The massacre was worse in the smaller cities and villages outside Dacca. A full-scale genocide was unfolding in the idyllic Bangladeshi countryside. There was trouble, a lot of trouble, in the land of lazy rivers.

These were times like no other in history. East and West Pakistan made up a country like no other in history. Separated by 1,800 kilometers, East and West shared little in common. They spoke different languages and had different cultures, customs, clothing, and food. Yet, when the British hastily left the Indian subcontinent, they artificially divided the sub-continent into two countries: the areas with a Muslim majority became Pakistan, and those areas with a Hindu majority formed India. The only problem was that the two pockets of the Muslim majority were located in the eastern and western corners of the Indian subcontinent. There was no land corridor between them. Hence, East and West Pakistan, though they were in theory one country, were separated by more than a thousand miles of hostile Indian land.

Figure 01: Map of East and West Pakistan

Over the years, tensions developed between the West Pakistanis and East Pakistanis (Bengalis). The Bengalis felt that the more powerful West Pakistanis controlled both the civil administration and the military and refused to give the East Pakistanis their fair share. They felt their language and culture were being replaced by a foreign ideology, and when the government declared that Urdu, a language spoken mostly by West Pakistanis, would be the national language replacing Bengali, the language of the Bengali people, as the medium of education in schools and colleges, there was widespread unrest. The two languages were different in script, phonetics, and structure, and the Bengalis were bitter that an alien language was being forced upon them. Bengalis took to the streets in protests, and there were Language Riots all over East Pakistan.

The Bengalis felt that, in the two decades following the partition of India, most of the resources were allocated to the West wing, whereas East Pakistan lagged behind in industrial development, infrastructure investment, and education. They believed that, compared with the more educated West Pakistanis, they were not given equal opportunity in jobs or business, and their people were bypassed when it came to promotions in civilian and military jobs. When the Bengalis demanded equal rights and representation, the West Pakistan military junta cracked down on them ruthlessly.

To make matters worse, when the tropical cyclone 'Bhola' caused widespread devastation in November of 1970, the central government, controlled mostly by West Pakistanis, failed to respond immediately. The woefully inadequate relief work resulted in a catastrophic number of casualties, marking Bhola as one of the deadliest natural disasters in recorded history. It was described as the deadliest tropical cyclone in history by the American Meteorological Society. The Bengalis blamed the West Pakistanis for the catastrophic loss of life, which they believed could have been prevented had the relief measures been implemented immediately. They were now convinced that they could no longer coexist with the West Pakistanis. They were determined to rid themselves of their Pakistani masters.

Finally, the last straw came when the Bengali presidential candidate, Sheikh Mujibur Rahman, was denied the presidency of a joint Pakistan, even though he won the elections fairly in December of 1970. His party, the Awami League, swept the elections but was not allowed to form the majority government that would rule the East and West halves of the country. The Bengalis were furious, and years of misgivings and unrest erupted into violent civil war. They no longer wanted to have anything to do with the West Pakistanis and declared independence in March 1971. The new country they envisioned was called Bangladesh, or 'The Land of Bengal'.

In this, the Indians saw an opportunity to score a victory against an erstwhile enemy. They had already fought two wars against Pakistan since gaining independence from Britain. Now, they openly supported the Bangladesh Liberation War and provided dissidents with arms and military training. The Pakistan Army tried to brutally quash the uprising, and in retaliation, the Bengali militia, known as the Mukti Bahini, began killing thousands of non-Bengalis. To them, Bangladesh was for Bengalis, and anyone who was not a Bengali was a Bihari and, therefore, not welcome. Unfortunately, we were among the Biharis.

The Abduls, our househelps, were among the Bengalis. I was quite sad that they had left, and without them, I felt very alone in our huge house. I went out to the backyard to play with my pet pigeon, Kabooter. I'd had six pigeons, but a few weeks ago, all but one of them had flown away. Perhaps they, too, had sensed the need to return to their families. Kabooter was the youngest and had stayed behind; he was very attached to me. Kabooter was quite big for his age and had the nicest pale brown and white velvety plume. I got out the feed, and he came and sat on my forearm as he pecked the seeds from my palm.

It was very quiet outside, too. I sat silently on the concrete steps leading down from our house, overlooking the water. The big pond behind our house was empty. No wooden dinghies skimmed the water, and I didn't see any fishermen throwing their nets either. The people who lived in the houses on the other side of the pond were missing, too. Nobody was out on our street, not even cars or autorickshaws. The neighborhood was eerily quiet. Kabooter and I sat for a long time together, and as the sun set behind the coconut trees on the other side of the pond, I went back inside.

2
Adamjee Nagar

Adamjee Nagar, or Adamjee Township, was a sprawling industrial complex located fourteen miles southeast of Dacca on the banks of the Sitalakkha River. Surrounded by fertile, jute-producing lands and with close access to the port city of Narayanganj, it was an ideal location for the Adamjee brothers to lay the foundations of the Adamjee Jute Mills in 1951.

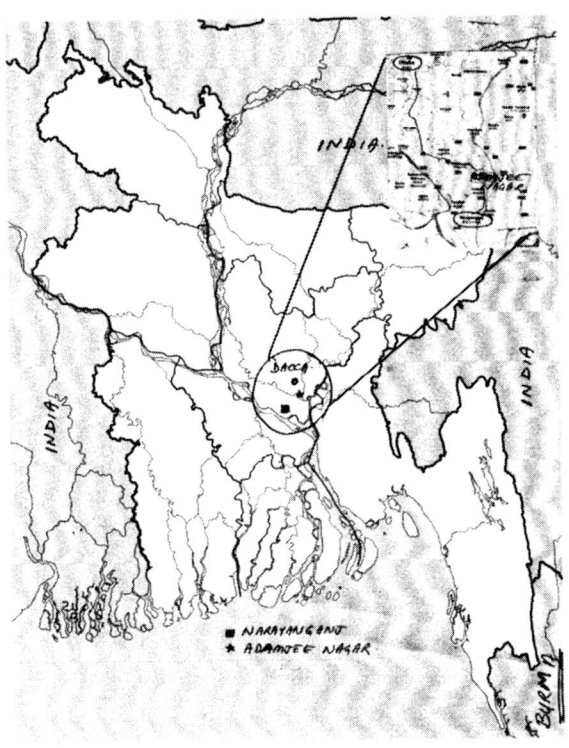

Figure 02: Map of East Pakistan

The industrial complex was a piece of the government's plan to bring heavy industries to East Pakistan. During the partition of India in 1947, there were more than one hundred jute mills in Bengal, but all were allocated to India. On the other hand, East Bengal, which became East Pakistan, received no heavy industries. In a plan to bring back economic equilibrium, the Pakistani government heavily subsidized the private sector in order to establish industries across East Pakistan. The Adamjee Jute Mills was the fruit of one such government-supported initiative.

Picture 04: Adamjee Jute Mills

The family-owned Adamjee Group of Companies acquired three hundred acres of land in the outskirts of Dacca and laid the foundation of the jute mills in 1951, thereby opening a new era of industrial development for the economically deprived East Pakistan. The mills' first looms started spinning in 1952, and soon afterward, my father joined the workforce.

In those days, jute, along with cotton, was the world's most widely used plant fiber and, perhaps, the cheapest. It was called the 'golden fiber', and before the advent of polypropylene, it was used extensively as a raw material in the construction industry, in the textile industry, and for packaging agricultural products. It was used for making bags, sacks, wrapping material, coarse cloth, curtains, area rugs, ropes, and other common household and industrial items.

The abundant jute crops in the fertile Bay of Bengal delta, along with efficient management by the entrepreneurial Adamjee brothers, soon made Adamjee Jute Mill the largest jute mill in the world, surpassing even those at Dundee and Calcutta. It was the pride of Pakistan's industrial development program and a must-see showpiece for all foreign dignitaries visiting East Pakistan. Pappa used to tell us of the time when Queen Elizabeth and the Duke of Edinburgh visited the mills.

By the late sixties, the Adamjee Jute Mills complex contained three mills with a combined three thousand loom capacity. The mills churned out thousands of tons of yarn, hessian fabric, and sacking bags. Pappa was a manager in Mill #3. Like Pappa, most of the mill managers and higher-level employees were Biharis. Biharis were among the more educated people who had emigrated from India after partition and, therefore, occupied the higher-paying positions in the mills. The Bengalis mostly held the lower-paying jobs as skilled or unskilled laborers, and this naturally created some resentment.

In its heyday, the Adamjee Jute Mills employed more than twenty thousand people who worked round the clock in shifts. The management staff lived on the riverfront or the talabs (large ponds), and the workers lived in housing quarters near the mills. Skilled workers lived in rows of workers' quarters surrounding the main shed of the jute mills, while many of the unskilled Bengali laborers lived in the nearby slums of Sumilpara. Others lived in shanties across the Sitalakkha River, which they crossed on bamboo rafts every morning.

Many Bengali laborers who worked in the mills kept their families in the villages and only visited them on holidays. They lived in poor conditions in overcrowded dorm-type rooms, sharing the space with laborers who worked different shifts. The workers' quarters were simple single-story buildings with tin roofs and barely any furniture except for rows of beds. They saved every penny they could to support their families back home in the villages. In those days, most villages in rural East Pakistan lacked electricity or running water. Agriculture and fishing were the predominant sources of income. Most families lived in mud houses with thatched roofs and traveled on boats or bullock carts. The common villagers were poor and lived hand to mouth.

My family lived in a sprawling house in the residential section for upper-level mill managers.

Picture 05: Our family on the front porch of our house in 1964

Fruit-laden banana and sweet-apple trees dotted the garden around our house, and tall coconut trees lined the perimeter. A dazzling array of dahlias and marigolds blossomed in the lush garden at the front of the house. The house was raised on a low foundation to prevent water damage. A few steps led up to the elevated porch that opened into the living room. Behind the living room was the kitchen on the right side and the children's bedroom on the left. Our bedroom directly opened into my parent's bedroom, whereas the kitchen backed up to a concrete backyard.

On the backside of our house was a large pond, the number 2 talab (or pond #2). Overlooking the pond and next to my parent's bedroom was our sunroom, which stood on wooden stilts at the water's edge. The sunroom was enclosed with woven wire mesh panels and had small windows from which my brother and I would dangle a fishing rod in summer.

Picture 06: Three siblings with the pond behind our house, 1967.

In the evenings, Ammi and Pappa would often relax in this room as they sipped their Bengali tea and watched the sunset. The gently flavored teas from the hillside tea gardens of Sylhet were considered some of the best in the world at par with those from Assam and Darjeeling. Underneath the sunroom was my chicken coop, and Abdul helped me take care of my pigeons and hens.

Pappa had a pigeon loft made for me next to the sunroom. It was a simple wood box with small cubicles for my six pigeons and was mounted on a tall wooden pole to keep them safe from predatory animals. To begin with, I had five pigeons, but then they laid eggs, and one day, a little one just magically hatched out from a tiny egg inside our loft. I named him Kabooter, and he was my favorite!

The hens lived in a much larger enclosure built of wood planks and meshed wire net. We would let the chickens out every afternoon to roam around the backyard. The roosters would grow very big, so much so that when they walked on the concrete floor of the backyard, one could hear an audible 'thud' as they put their feet down. They were very colorful and would grow beautiful, shiny plumes and bright red crowns.

I used to spend hours playing with my pet chickens and pigeons after coming home from school.

I was a skinny, lanky, and energetic eight-year-old boy. Ammi used to dress me up in short pants and crisply ironed short-sleeved shirts. I used to slant my hair down my forehead because that's how one of the famous movie stars wore his hair in those days. I loved to put on a peaked police hat and carry my toy gun and holster. I fantasized about becoming a police officer. I was happy-go-lucky, carefree, and playful, unlike Khusro Bhaijan, who had started taking his studies more seriously.

Picture 07: Three siblings with Aunt in 1969; I am the youngest.

Khusro Bhaijan was four years older than me and much more sober and well-composed. He was studious and got good grades in school. Bhaijan was very smart and clever too, and Ammi used to say he carried a 'good head on his shoulders'. He graduated from the Narayanganj Preparatory English School in 1970 and had started middle school at the prestigious Shaheen Academy in Dacca, run by the Pakistan Air Force. He used to go to his new school smartly dressed up in his maroon blazer, khaki pants, and striped, maroon, and yellow tie. My sister, Maliha Apa, and I used to look up to him. My grandmother, when she visited us from India, told us, "Khusro is the train engine of your family; you two are the little bogies. You just follow the engine, and you will get to the right station!"

Picture 08: Grandparents visiting from India in 1969

Maliha Apa was two years older than me. Ammi loved to dress her up in pretty frocks all the time and did her hair in all kinds of fashionable arrangements. She was the little princess of our family. The three of us shared a room just outside Ammi and Pappa's bedroom. Every night, Ammi would have us brush our teeth, put us in our beds, and then retire to her room.

Picture 09: Khusro Bhaijan, Maliha Apa, and me.

In the afternoon, I would play with my pets, and then I would go out to play games with the neighborhood kids. Tutul lived across the street from me, and he was the son of my father's Bengali manager, Mr. Chowdhury. Mostly, we played cricket or rode our bikes. The street in front of our house was a cul-de-sac, so there was not much traffic, and we could play safely. Our neighbors were both Bihari and Bengali officers at the mill. Many were Bengalis, and we played with their children and visited their houses regularly. We never felt there was any difference between them and us.

After sundown, I would watch television with my family. In those days, the black-and-white transmission started at 6 p.m. with the playing of the national anthem and the recitation of the Holy Quran. I remember watching TV shows like *The Avengers, Saint, Invisible Man, The Fugitive, Lassie, I Love Lucy, Bonanza, Star Trek, Get Smart,* and *Bewitched*. My favorite character was Mr. Spock from *Star Trek* and, of course, the collie dog, Lassie. I even remember watching the black and white recording of the moon landing in late July of 1969. The TV room was in the front of the house, and after watching a few shows, we would go to the adjoining kitchen, which faced the backyard. The kitchen was a small room with barely a few closets, a small kitchen table, an aerated Hawadaan (a ventilated wooden cabinet used to keep meat and other edibles fresh) on the back side, and a kerosene stove in one corner.

Dinner was always served in the dining room, and Ammi and Abdul would have to pull us out of the TV room to start dinner. Abdul was a good cook, and his warm rotis fresh off the stove were delicious. After dinner, Ammi would change us and put us in bed. But not before the most dreaded deal of the day. Before bed, all three of us were given a tablespoon of the dreaded Seven Seas Cod Liver Oil. My parents were so convinced of the health benefits of malted cod liver oil that they never spared us from taking it, even after we threw up many times trying to gulp it down!

My mother loved to cook for us. My favorite food was Khubuli (layered rice and lentils) and the English pudding cooked under boiling water. But she loved making Bengali cuisine the most. With Abdul's help, she would make Hilsa, Rohu, and all kinds of Bengali fish and serve them with rice. She used to say that Bengali kids in our school were brainy because they ate fish, and she was determined to make all three of us eat as much fish as she could. The only problem was that I hated fish!

The community of Adamjee Nagar was surrounded by an eight-foot-high wall that was pale yellow and stained. A towering gatepost was made of slender concrete columns with a crossbar at the top, which welcomed visitors to the compound. The Adamjee Jute Mills crest, placed at the center of the gatepost, proudly boasted the might of the private industrial empire. Massive mill sheds occupied the back of the compound, nearer the river, and the living quarters were located closer toward the entrance and the narrow two-way road leading to Dacca. Tall godowns separated the mills from the living quarters and functioned as a sound barrier. A single-track railway line and a jetty on the Sitalakkha River provided means of transporting the finished jute products out of Adamjee Nagar.

Picture 10: Adamjee Jute Mills Entrance

Adamjee Nagar was developed as a self-contained community with its own police station, post office, and mosque. There was even a tennis club, a playground, and numerous ponds (talabs). But there was no shopping center or school.

The dull hum of machinery, spinning wheels, and weaving shuttles permeated the air in Adamjee Nagar and was only broken by the melancholic siren announcing the shift change for mill workers. Apart from the three jute mills and the homes of those who worked in the mills, there was not much else in the compound. For most of our daily needs and shopping, we used to travel five miles to the city of Narayanganj.

In the early seventies, Narayanganj was a small town located on the banks of the Sitalakkha River and served as the main port for the city of Dacca. The finished jute products from Adamjee Jute Mills arrived at the port on barges and trains and were then loaded onto ships and transported all over the world. Old colonial-style, two-story townhouses lined both sides of the streets, while most of the light industries and warehouses were located close to the riverbanks.

I was born in the Holy Family Hospital in Narayanganj and later went to Narayanganj Preparatory English School, the same school my older siblings attended. When I started school in 1967, my sister was two years ahead of me, and my brother was four years my senior. It was a private English-medium elementary school up to six grade levels only, so by the time I reached third grade, my brother had already graduated and started middle school at the Shaheen Academy in Dacca.

Narayanganj Preparatory English School was located in the heart of the old town and surrounded by residential buildings. The double-story colonial-style school building was quite small, and there was barely a small playground. It was run by an all-female staff. Most of the staff was Bengali, but a few of the teachers were Bihari or Anglicans. My headmistress was a tall, broad-built, English-speaking lady from Scotland, Mrs. Hubbard. She was very fair-skinned and wore long skirts. She looked very big in the small corridors and rooms of our school.

I loved going to school and playing with my friends. My friend Fayaz and I used to sit together at our desks in the front row. He was dark, skinny, and quiet. His mother, Mrs. Khatoon, taught us religion during the third period. We also studied mathematics, sociology, and history, but arts were my favorite subject; I loved drawing cartoons. Ammi also taught English to elementary school students at the Narayanganj Preparatory English School, and the best part was that she was my class teacher in the second grade. It was great fun to have Ammi as my class teacher. On occasions, she would take me and my sister to the teacher's lounge during lunch break, and that made us feel very important.

Ammi was the daughter of a high-ranking civil servant in the princely state of Hyderabad Deccan, where she was born and raised. Her father was a collector (Talukdar) in the government of the Nizam of Hyderabad. She went to the Women's College and then completed her bachelor's degree in home economics. She was the oldest of eight siblings, which probably taught her to be calm and self-composed under stress. After her marriage, she moved to Adamjee Nagar, a year after Pappa joined the Adamjee Jute Mills. Together, they had three children; I was the youngest. She stayed home and looked after the three of us until we were of school-going age. Once I enrolled in the Narayanganj Preparatory English School, she also joined the teaching staff.

Picture 11: My mother (Ammi)

Pappa was in his early forties and in the prime of his life when I started going to school. He was stocky, muscular, and athletic, an avid sportsman. In college, he had been a member of the soccer, wrestling, and weightlifting teams. He had traveled all over India as the captain of the City College and later the Osmania University soccer team. The TV room in our house was full of trophies and plaques he had won. After finishing college in Hyderabad Deccan, India, he immigrated to East Pakistan in 1957 and found an entry-level job at the Adamjee Jute Mills. Once he had settled in his new job, he went back to Hyderabad to marry Ammi, and the two settled in Adamjee Nagar to start a new life. By virtue of his hard work and his excellent work ethic, he quickly climbed the ladder and became a manager at Mill #3 at a very early age.

Picture 12: My father (Pappa)

Early each morning, Pappa would drive the four of us to school in our navy blue 1967 Fiat 1100. Ammi would sit in the front passenger seat, and the three of us would sit in the back. I loved the brown leather seats and the rustic smell of dry, parched leather. This was my favorite time of the day.

The short road trip would take us over the many lazy rivers, oxbow lakes, and canals crisscrossing the land around Narayanganj and past banana and pineapple plantations on either side of the road. I loved rolling down my rear door glass and letting the moisture-laden wind from the rivers graze my face.

Looking outside my car window, I would marvel at the incredibly lush, green, and beautiful scenery.

Picture 13: Land of the Lazy Rivers

Abundant green shoots sprouted from the land all around, and evergreen bamboo bundles grew like wildfire between flooded paddy rice fields.

The monsoon season brought heavy loads of rain, which fed the rivers and filled the ponds, lakes, and rivulets to the brim. From here, the water lazily continued its southward journey. This is where the stampeding waters of the mighty Ganges and Brahmaputra, having lost their ferocity, drained slowly and unceremoniously into the Bay of Bengal through innumerable serpentine distributaries.

Driving along the road, one could see the boatmen throwing their nets into the river to catch fish. Some boats had sails, others had canopy covers, and still others were simple wooden dinghies or Sampans. Boats were not only used as modes of transportation in inland waterways, but many Bengali fishermen also lived on their boats. For many Bengalis, the river was their lifeline. The Majhi, or boatmen, and their boats were part of the folklore and the subjects of songs and ballads that praised their way of life. Bhatiyali is the folk music of Bengal, a 'boat song' or 'river song' sung by boatmen as they sail down streams of the river.

> *O' boatman, O' boatman,*
> *Whether a storm rages,*
> *Whether rainclouds rumble,*
> *Take us across to the other end, O' boatman.*
> *However loud these river torrents roar,*
> *Help me get my boat to the shore.*
> *Take us across to the other end, O' boatman,*
> *O' boatman, O' boatman.*

The long-drawn-out high notes of the Bhatiyali songs, meandering into low tones, left a haunting yet serene mark on anyone who ever came across this beautiful music. Often sung solo by the boatman, the songs tell of their lone journey down the vast, never-ending river. They tell about the bountiful harvests the river brings but also about the drudgery of the journey, the treacherous river, the storms and floods, and the Majhi's everlasting quest for the shore.

After school, we would sometimes go to the open-air Shonar Bangla market. The bazaars were always so overcrowded that the rickshaw pullers rubbed shoulders with the shoppers. One could buy anything here, including colorful jamdani saris, pottery, handicrafts, spices, fruits, vegetables, and the famous Bengali sweets. My favorites were the Bengali Doi and Roshogolla. This is where I had bought my pet pigeons and chickens. The Bengalis loved fish, and we could buy every kind of fish at the market.

On some weekends, we would visit the historic Sonargaon in Narayanganj to enjoy nature. We would take a boat ride or visit the museum. The Dacca Racecourse grounds and Dhanmondi Lake were other places we would go for picnics. Abdul would prepare some of the most delicious sandwiches and carry them in a cane basket. I remember spreading out a sheet on plush green grass and eating fresh native fruits like lychee, pineapple, and jackfruit. My favorite was the lychee with its delicious, juicy flesh inside the prickly skin. On our way back, we would often get Igloo ice cream from the shopping complex at the Baitul-Mukarram Mosque in Dacca.

Often, we would visit our family in Dacca on holidays or weekends. Adamjee Nagar was a very small community, and most of the people we knew lived in Dacca. So, going to Dacca to visit our friends or family was always a treat, and we made use of every opportunity to go there. My cousin Ashraf lived in Dacca, and we would go to his house to play hide and seek or board games like Ludo and Snakes and Ladders late into the nights. I remember that in early 1971 my family was planning to go to Ashraf's house to spend the Bakra Eid weekend. The day before, Ashraf's dad had come to visit us for some errand, and after a great deal of cajoling, my parents consented to allow me to go with her to Dacca ahead of the planned family visit. In my frenzied excitement, I ran out of the kitchen to gather my clothes, stumbled on the concrete stairs, and chipped my front tooth. Needless to say, on that particular occasion, we did not go to Dacca.

Adamjee Nagar was far enough away from Dacca to be free from the hustle and bustle of the big city. Other than the mills and the houses of those who worked here, there was not much to the sleepy township of Adamjee Nagar. Only the mill workers and their families lived in the area, and nothing much ever happened. Life was very simple, peaceful, and even laid-back.

But for the last few months, trouble had been brewing, even in this idyllic community. In October 1971, the Awami League, the party of Mujibur Rahman, who had won the elections and yet denied power, organized a violent demonstration inside the compound. Bengali mill workers armed with bamboo sticks and lathis attacked the central office of Adamjee Jute Mills. The Pakistan Army used teargas to disperse the demonstrators and arrested many Bengalis. In early December, the bodies of five young Bengali laborers were found in a ditch near Mill #3. No one knew who had killed them. The Bengali mill workers were becoming increasingly queasy. Many had left their jobs and ran away to their villages outside Dacca and away from the reach of the dreaded Pakistani Army. Abdul had known one of the dead mill workers as he was from the same village. He panicked and decided to leave abruptly, too, but he did so with a heavy heart.

Now, there was an ominous uneasiness in the air. The street outside our house looked deserted. Our Bengali neighbors no longer greeted us, and my Bengali friends wouldn't come out to play with me. It was a strange feeling.

3
Amar Shonar Bangla

Amar shonar Bangla.
Ami tomae bhalobashi.

Sang all the Abduls in a chorus. They would gather under the lamppost in front of my house after they'd finished their daily chores, and they would talk about old times and their families and villages back home. They would tell enchanting tales of farmers plowing in the vast, verdant fields or of the Majhis rowing their boats in the innumerous lazy rivers and canals, interlacing the riverine delta. Sometimes, they would play mellow tunes on the flute and serenade late into the night:

Amar shonar Bangla. Ami tomae bhalobashi.
O! My beloved Bengal of gold. You are my love.

It was a beautiful and melodious song, and the Bengalis were a nation of devout music lovers. The melodious tune permeating the midnight air made one instantly fall in love with the musical and magical land that was Bengal.

These were the 'Abduls' of Adamjee Nagar. They worked in the neighboring houses as cooks, guards, gardeners, or caretakers. Abdul was a very common first name in Bengal in those days, and many of these househelps were named Abdul. I remember there was an 'Abdul' in almost every house in my neighborhood. Abdul Mannan, Abdul Rahman, Abdul Rahim, so on and so forth. The name Abdul derives from the Arabic root word meaning 'servant' and was originally meant to mean 'servant of Manan', 'servant of Rahman', etc., which are all attributes of God. But in our community, it became almost a synonym for the servant househelps in Adamjee Nagar. We were dependent upon the Abduls for all our house chores.

The Abduls had come to Adamjee Nagar from the small villages and towns surrounding Dacca in search of work. Many had found work in the Adamjee Jute Mills as laborers, but those who found work as househelps were considered better off since they at least had better accommodations. They lived in small quarters in their employers' households but kept their families in villages and only visited them on their days off. Like those who worked in the factories, they saved every penny they could from their meager income to send home to their families in the villages.

Our Abdul came from the Noakhali District of Bengal. He worked for us, yes, but he had been with our family for such a long time that we thought of him almost as a family member. He cooked, cleaned, and took care of us, and when we came home from school, he played with us in the backyard or kept an eye on me as I played with my pets. In the evening, he would bring me hot milk as I played outside.

Abdul spoke in broken Urdu but with a heavy Bengali accent, kind of an interesting mix of Urdu and Bengali. He was a thin, dark-skinned, and petite man with a short scruffy goatee. He was very soft-spoken and friendly. Like most of the Abduls, he wore a half-sleeve shirt over a brightly colored, checkered, traditional Bengali lungi, a long piece of cloth that he wrapped around his waist. He was dependable and trustworthy.

And he was fun too! He showed me how to cut a banana from our garden into two pieces without even peeling the skin. He would encircle a threaded needle through all the corners of the banana peel and pull the string out from the entry site. This would leave the skin intact but cut the pulp into two. Then I would peel away the intact skin and find two neatly cut pieces inside! It was pure magic.

In the late sixties and early seventies, the general mood in East Pakistan was that of disenfranchisement of the Bengalis due to their heavy-handed treatment by the West Pakistanis. Common people were becoming increasingly frustrated and resentful, and this feeling was reflected in the changing attitudes of the Abduls. They were angry about the injustices occurring in East Pakistan, but, at the same time, they were confused. These Abduls were simple folk from the villages and could not reconcile their positive interactions with their Bihari employers against the brutal actions of the Pakistan Army.

Over the last few months, during their late-night gatherings under the lampposts, the Abduls had been talking about more serious matters, such as politics, liberation from the Pakistanis, and the independence of Bangladesh. In these last few months, they were talking enthusiastically about the political meetings and rallies organized by the Awami League.

Picture 14: Mass Demonstrations

These days, there was a new meaning to 'Amar Shonar Bangla'. The song had become the anthem of a movement for change. It seemed to have taken on a more nationalistic undertone, implying that Bengal is for the Bengalis and that the Biharis, the usurpers of Bengali rights, were not welcome. Suddenly, the melodious song had become rather unnerving and carried an almost ominous tone for us.

The Abduls were also attending political meetings organized by the Awami League. The Awami League, headed by Sheikh Mujibur Rahman, had won ninety-nine percent of the popular vote in East Pakistan in the 1970 election but had been prevented from forming a majority government that would rule over the entire united Pakistan.

In the western wing of the country, The Peoples Party, led by Zulfiqar Ali Bhutto, bagged 81 parliamentary seats. In comparison, the Awami League had won 160 seats, mostly from the more populous East. Clearly, the Awami League should have been asked to form government and Mujibur Rahman should have become the prime minister of both parts of the country, but the West Pakistanis found it inconceivable that they would be ruled by an East Pakistani, whom they considered inferior. Zulfiqar Ali Bhutto saw an opportunity to grab power through the back door in West Pakistan, declaring, "*Udhar tum aur idhar hum* (You, there and us, here)."

A statement that clearly insinuated dividing the country along geographic and ethnic grounds and, ultimately, cemented the breakup of the country into two halves.

One day, our Abdul came home very late after an Awami League rally. He was very excited.

"Bibiji! You 'bhill' see 'Bongabandhu' 'bhill' be the prime minister of Pakistan 'bhery' soon, and then 'overything' will be all right."

Bangabandhu was the title given to Mujibur Rahman and meant 'Friend of Bengal'.

Ammi acted surprised. "Where did you hear that, Abdul?"

"In the Awami League rally I 'ent' to in Sumilpara!" Abdul said proudly.

"They told all the mill workers 'bhill' not talk in Urdu bhasha anymore. From today, I bhill not speak with any Bihari in Urdu," he declared decisively. Urdu was a language of the Biharis.

"How would you, then, talk to us?"

"Oh…!" Abdul seemed perplexed at this seemingly simple question but made a quick comeback, "I 'bhill' talk to you in Urdu; you are 'phamily', Bibiji!"

In the months leading up to December 1971, rallies and labor strikes were organized in Adamjee Nagar. The mill workers were becoming very angry and even hostile. Pappa worried about the rapidly worsening situation in the mills, where the workers were growing increasingly rowdy and disruptive. He couldn't believe how fast their attitude had changed and lamented that everyone in Adamjee Nagar, including his old friends and neighbors, was turning away from him. Pappa was an ordinary citizen with no political affiliations, and he was just working hard to make an honest living in East Pakistan. But he felt he was being singled out because he was not a Bengali.

One day, while returning from work on his bicycle, Pappa was confronted by an angry crowd of laborers, who accused him of being a collaborator of the Pakistan Army just because he was a Bihari and, therefore, assumed to be in cahoots with the Pakistan Army. From there on, fearing for his safety, Pappa began driving to work.

Our Abduls also took part in these rallies, which were organized by the Awami League and openly demanded freedom from Pakistan. Many of these rallies turned into riots, at which point the Pakistani Army would come and indiscriminately arrest the Bengali mill workers. Many of our Abduls went into hiding or fled to their villages to escape the Pakistan Army. Our house guard, 'Little Abdul', had run away a few days ago to escape persecution at the hands of the army. On 3 December 1971, Abdul, our long-time househelp, had to leave us as well.

4
Ides of March

Nine months earlier, in March 1971, the Bengalis repaid their debt to the West Pakistanis in blood. The Mukti Bahini went on a killing spree across East Pakistan. A rampaging gang of miscreants attacked a sister factory of Adamjee Jute Mills, which was close to my elementary school in Narayanganj, and slaughtered the Bihari employees indiscriminately.

In Chittagong, a Bengali mob beat up my friend Salahuddin Ayubi's father and left him for dead. He was barely alive when an astute doctor saw some signs of life and resuscitated him. He suffered multiple head and limb injuries, and when the doctor revived him, he was in shock, disoriented, and unable to remember anything. Luckily, a distant Bengali acquaintance recognized him and brought him home.

My friend Aamir Syed was only 11 years old when his father, a journalist in the Chittagong Morning News, boarded a train on 23rd of March to go to Dacca. The train was forcibly stopped at Bhairab Bazar, where elements of Mukti Bahini ordered all the non-Bengalis to disembark. His father was among the two hundred and fifty Urdu-speaking passengers who were forcibly taken away and imprisoned in a tea company warehouse. A few days later, they were paraded to a bridge in Brahmanbaria, where they were all beheaded and their bodies were thrown into the river.

In Dacca, a number of Bengali soldiers in the Pakistan Army mutinied and killed their senior Bihari officers. Pappa's close friend, Major Rabb, was shot point-blank by his own troops when he came out of his quarters to investigate the commotion in the middle of the night. His wife and young son only narrowly escaped. Pappa was very worried, and I didn't quite know what to make out of it. I wondered what would happen now to my young friend. I was confused and puzzled, and all my guts felt topsy-turvy.

That same month, the Mukti Bahini attacked the Karnaphuli Paper Mills in Chittagong and killed more than three hundred Bihari men. My friend Fasih Soherwardy's dad was a manager in the mills and was taken for interrogation. He was tortured and killed; his body was placed in a jute bag weighted with stones and thrown into the Karnaphuli River. The Bihari women and children were locked in the tennis court clubhouse for days without water or food before they were shot and killed by indiscriminate firing. My ten-year-old friend was one of only six survivors.

When news of the Bihari massacre at Karnaphuli reached West Pakistan, the Pakistani dictator, General Yahya Khan, was furious.

"Kill three million of them, and they will eat out of our hands," he is reported to have said. Inferring how a tame, domesticated animal would eat out of their master's hand.

The Pakistan Army came down on the Bengalis with an iron fist and launched the infamous 'Operation Searchlight' on the night of 25th of March.

In the dark of the night, the Bengali independence movement leader Sheikh Mujibur Rahman was captured from his home in Dacca by military commandos and secretly flown to West Pakistan, where he was imprisoned. The Bengali militant strongholds were raided, and thousands were arrested. Entire Bengali neighborhoods were set on fire. The Awami League was outlawed, and the offices of Bengali newspapers were ransacked. That same night, the Pakistan Army violently seized control of Dacca University, killing two hundred Bengali student activists.

The mastermind behind Operation Searchlight was Lt. General Tikka Khan of the Pakistan Army, who had arrived in Dacca just a few weeks ago as the new chief of the Eastern Command. His predecessor, Lt. General Sahibzada Yaqub Ali Khan, had left abruptly, unable to carry on with the brutal treatment of Bengalis demanded by his higher-ups. But Tikka Khan was a different general, and he was determined to quench the rebellion at all costs. A ruthless man who would soon earn the nickname 'The Butcher of Bengal'.

The violent Operation Searchlight unleashed a reign of terror that lasted two months and resulted in looting and the maiming and slaughter of the Bengali population. From Rajshahi to Chittagong, from Mymensingh to Barisal, and from Sylhet to Jessore, East Pakistan was burning. Pakistani soldiers raided and pillaged villages and towns to forcibly restore government control. Women were raped, and children were orphaned. Bengalis were killed at even the slightest suspicion that they supported the Bangladesh independence movement. Hindu Bengalis were assumed to be supporters of India and were killed on sight.

Some Bihari civilians assisted the Pakistan Army to quell the rebellion and wipe out the separatist elements. A small group of Bengalis who supported a united Pakistan also took part in this carnage.

The Mukti Bahini, now aided openly by India, retaliated, and East Pakistan spiraled into a full-scale civil war.

With the situation rapidly deteriorating, my father decided to move our family to safety, and in April 1971, we left East Pakistan and flew over to West Pakistan. Here, we stayed with Ammi's second cousin, Mr. Samdani. He was a kind man, a few years older than my parents, and he was like a big brother to them. While my parents had migrated to East Pakistan after the partition of India, he had migrated to West Pakistan and lived here with his wife and four children, who were a little older than me.

During our stay in Karachi, Pappa went to the Adamjee Industries headquarters and tried his best to get a permanent transfer to one of the Adamjee factories in West Pakistan. His request was denied. Rather, he was told that Operation Searchlight had restored law and order to East Pakistan and that the situation was getting better on the ground. In fact, he was told to report back to the Adamjee Jute Mills immediately.

Pappa was hesitant in returning to East Pakistan, and every day, there would be endless discussions about what should be done next. One day, Pappa suddenly said, "Maybe I would go back to work in Adamjee Nagar alone while the family stays back in Karachi."

"No, no, no!" Mr. Samdani said as he shifted uneasily in his sofa. "It's too dangerous to go to East Pakistan; it is best for you and your family to stay here in Karachi until the dust settles down in Dacca." He was wearing a white kurta and pajama, and for a moment, he looked as pale as his white dress.

"And what about the children's school in Narayanganj and the education they are missing?" Ammi sounded worried as she looked at Khusro Bhaijan, Maliha Apa, and me. The three of us sat cross-legged on the carpet, trying to comprehend what was going on.

"Perhaps we should rent a home here and put the children in school." Pappa was really trying hard to convince Ammi.

"My home is always open for you and your family; you need not worry about renting a place," said Mr. Samdani as he adjusted his thick glasses on his face. "Maybe you can even find a job here."

"But I can't leave my job with Adamjee; I will lose my seniority and pension that I have worked so hard for." Pappa was clearly dismayed as he slumped back into his chair.

"I wish I had come to West Pakistan like you did right from the beginning," Pappa lamented.

"Qumaruddin Bhaijan! Hindsight is always 20/20; who would have known things would turn out like this?" Mr. Samdani tried to console my father.

In the living room of his one-story house in Shareefabad, Karachi, Ammi, Pappa, and Mr. Samdani spent hours discussing possible solutions until one evening Ammi put her foot down.

"I have decided we all have to stay together, and if you are going to Dacca, we are all coming with you."

Ammi had made up her mind.

Pappa was hesitant but could not bear to argue with her.

"We haven't done anything wrong to the Bengalis; they should not target us." She was quite adamant. "We are civilians and have nothing to do with the army or their behavior."

After spending three months in the doldrums in West Pakistan, my family flew back to Dacca in July 1971.

While we were returning to Dacca, many of our friends and family were getting out of Dacca.

My cousin Ashraf lived in the Dhanmondi neighborhood of Dacca. Though he was a couple of years older, we played well together. On holidays, I would spend a few days at his home.

Ashraf was an only child, so my aunt and uncle doted on him and granted him his every wish. Needless to say, he had an enormous collection of toys, and in his huge collection were many toy soldiers, guns, tanks, and fighter planes. We used to play with these toys and thoroughly enjoyed beating the Indian soldiers in our make-believe war games. We used to joke about how cowardly the Indian soldiers were and that each of our brave Pakistani soldiers was better than ten Indians. The Mukti Bahini, we were not sure about though. We were very scared of them and afraid to talk about them. We had heard horror stories of what the Mukti Bahini could do.

His father used to work at the Standard Chartered Bank. When the situation in East Pakistan became dangerous, he was able to get a transfer to a branch of the same bank in West Pakistan. In August 1971, my cousin Ashraf and his family left Dacca forever. I was very sad.

My father's older cousin, Azmatulla uncle, was a senior vice president at the Habib Bank in Dacca. Pappa used to look up to him as a family elder, and we used to go to his house almost every other week. He was a very successful man and Pappa's role model. He lived in an upscale neighborhood in Dacca with his wife and three children, Razi Bhai, Rani Apa, and Savez. We loved going to their house and spending time with them. He also transferred to West Pakistan in early 1971, and our family felt quite isolated in East Pakistan.

Over the next few months, the Pakistani military sent more and more reinforcements to control the worsening situation in East Pakistan. Entire brigades of the Punjab Regiment, Baloch Regiment, and Frontier Force were flown in from West Pakistan. At the same time, there was a mass exodus of Bihari civilians out of East Pakistan. They fled by whatever mode of transportation they could find to get out of this quagmire. Air travel was available to only a few through the national courier, Pakistan International Airlines, because the flights were very infrequent. India no longer allowed Pakistani aircraft to fly over their airspace, so planes headed for Karachi, West Pakistan, had to take a long and circuitous route over the Bay of Bengal, the Indian Ocean, and the Arabian Sea. It required a stop in Ceylon to refuel, and the flight was not only very long but very expensive.

Many civilians found space in the merchant navy ships that were returning to West Pakistan after bringing military reinforcements and supplies. Shams, Safina e Arab, Ocean Endurance, and Ohrmazd were some of the merchant navy ships that took part in the evacuation. The ships would leave Chittagong Port and make a stopover at Colombo, Ceylon, before proceeding to Karachi.

It took seven days to get to Karachi. These ships were often overbooked and overcrowded, with many passengers crammed into small cabins. Some even traveled by cargo ships and on ship decks to escape from East Pakistan.

Others escaped across the border to Burma on land or on small boats and found refuge in the Pakistani Embassy in Rangoon. My friend Aamair Syed and his widowed mother spent a week in a tented refugee camp before smugglers took them across the border into Burma. Many other Biharis fled north into Nepal, and from there, they were airlifted to West Pakistan. It was chaos all around.

The West Pakistani military junta masterminded and executed the plan to arrest, terrorize, and kill the Bengali politicians, intellectuals, student leaders, and even the Bengali personnel of their own armed forces. They had hoped that by taking out the leadership of the nationalist movement, the separatist sentiments would die down, but the atrocities committed during this brutal campaign only led to popular uprising across the land of Bengal. By the autumn of 1971, nearly the entire Bengali nation had risen against the West Pakistanis. It was clear that a mere hundred thousand Pakistani soldiers and their two million Bihari sympathizers would not be able to control a population of more than sixty-six million Bengalis. Most of the country slipped out of their hands. The Pakistani Army only controlled some pockets of the larger cities, where they continued their heavy-handed treatment of the native population.

During the brutal crackdown, many Bengalis fled to small villages out of the army's reach. Thousands fled across the border to safe havens in India, and hundreds of thousands of Bengalis were uprooted from their homes and became refugees. Factories and businesses were closed due to unrest, and millions had lost their livelihood. East Pakistan plunged even further into poverty.

By the fall of 1971, almost the entire East Wing of Pakistan had come to a standstill. My school was closed indefinitely. The doors of Adamjee Jute Mills were shut as the plant lost running water and electricity. We no longer heard the constant hum of the machinery or the shift change sirens three times a day. There was an ominous silence in the air in Adamjee Nagar.

Like many poor Bengalis, our househelps, the Abduls, were from small villages around Dacca. They worked in cities for a meager income, and their families lived hand to mouth in villages. These impoverished and poverty-stricken Bengalis suffered the most during the turmoil. Abdul was our loyal employee for more than a decade, and he loved us. He did not want to part with us. He was sorry that he had to leave us when we felt vulnerable, but with the conditions deteriorating, Abdul had no choice but to go home and take care of his family in the village.

5
The War

The day was 3rd of December 1971. The evening was dull and gray. Dark wintery clouds hovered over our house and the pond, making the evening duskier than usual for this time of the day. The wind was holding its breath as if waiting in anticipation for something to happen. Not a leaf ruffled, nor a bird flew.

Abdul had just left abruptly for his village, and for the first time, there was no staff at home. The house felt different and uneasy. Ammi and Pappa did not sip their evening tea in the sunroom that evening. My friends did not come out to play either. With Abdul gone, I didn't get my usual cup of warm milk either as I played outside with my only remaining pet pigeon, Kabooter. I stayed for a while in the backyard and then went inside. It was quite an empty feeling.

Ammi and Pappa both looked worried that evening. They did not talk much. They briefly told us that a war had started between Pakistan and India earlier that afternoon. I did not quite understand what war was. Ammi told me we would all sleep in her room, which made me quite happy, as it was a treat for us to get to sleep in Ammi and Pappa's room. I thought war must not be too bad.

We ate dinner quietly without Abdul for the first time. It was strange not to have him around. Pappa put on Akashvani Agartala station from All India Radio. The newscaster was charged, talking very fast and rhetorically. He said a full-scale war had broken out between India and Pakistan on both the western and eastern fronts. The announcer claimed that Indian military forces would inflict a deadly blow to Pakistan and break our country into two, thus liberating the Bengalis from West Pakistani occupation. I thought that did not sound nice or polite.

Later that night, we woke up to the sound of loud sirens coming from the jute mills. I was puzzled as I knew it was not the time for shift change at the mills, and the siren was louder than usual. Pappa and Ammi took the three of us, and we all ducked under the big bed. After the sirens came the frightening sounds of military aircraft, which were immediately followed by explosions like I had never heard before. It was terrifyingly loud. Minutes later, the crackling sound of anti-aircraft guns filled the air. It, too, was frighteningly loud. It sounded like vicious animals were gnarling and tearing each other apart. I was very scared.

The next day, 4 December 1971, the Indian Air Force bombarded Adamjee Jute Mills again, and this time, the bombs hit one of the residential areas of Adamjee Nagar. We heard that many civilian mill workers died during the airstrike.

The same day, the president of Pakistan, General Yahya Khan, spoke to the nation. We tried to fix antennas onto our boxed black-and-white Phillips television set, hoping to catch the signal, but transmissions from Pakistani television in Dacca had probably already been suspended. So, we gathered around our old, polished veneer radiogram. Yahya Khan was very upbeat, too, and boastfully promised that the Pakistan Army would resoundingly defeat the Indians on all fronts. He said, "Our lion-hearted jawans blew away the Indians in the 1965 war, and this time, we would hit them even harder."

Such was the propaganda we were listening to in those days. In reality, the Indian Army had infiltrated the border in massive numbers almost a month ago, and along with the Mukti Bahini, it now controlled most of the Bangladeshi countryside. The Pakistan Army had been mostly confined to larger cities and cantonment areas.

That night, we slept in Ammi and Papa's room again. There was pitch-black darkness. Electricity to our house had been cut off earlier in the day. At night, we heard sporadic gunfire and more distant bombardment by the Indian Air Force. We locked our house from the inside. We were afraid that the Mukti Bahini might attack us, and without our security guard, Little Abdul, we felt very vulnerable. We had heard many Bihari houses had been attacked by Mukti Bahini in and around Adamjee Nagar. We didn't sleep much that night either.

The next morning, we sat for breakfast around the kitchen table. Pappa took out Dabal Roti and jam from the aerated Hawadaan closet and said it was too dangerous to live in Adamjee Nagar anymore. We had to leave. Ammi was surprised.

"Where will we go?" she asked as she prepared breakfast for us.

"You remember Mr. Huq, we met at Major Rabb's funeral?" Pappa said. "He lives in the Dacca Cantonment. Maybe we should go over there until the war is over, and then we come back."

"But do we know them well enough? Have you talked to him about us coming over?" Ammi asked.

"The phone lines are down. I tried calling him this morning," Pappa said as he spread a thick layer of jam on my toast. "But the last time we met, he did ask me to come over to the cantonment if the situation became dangerous in Adamjee Nagar."

"I worry about Adamjee Nagar, too. We are far from the city, and I am afraid that it might fall into the hands of Mukti Bahini."

"Not just that!" Pappa sounded even more worried. "Adamjee Jute Mills is one of the biggest industrial complexes in East Pakistan, so Adamjee Nagar is a prime target for Indian Air Force bombardment during this war."

"And what about our home?"

"We will worry about that later," Pappa said hastily. "I am really worried about our safety here. Let's pack and leave quickly."

By this time, Ammi was looking really scared as Pappa tried to calm her down.

"There is a big contingent of the Pakistan Army in the cantonment; we would be quite safe there during the war," Pappa said. "If God wills, we will be back home soon!"

Pappa had lived through the 1965 war between India and Pakistan. The war was mostly fought at the border, and there was almost no trouble in Adamjee Nagar. Both Bengalis and Biharis had fought side by side against India. But now, the Bengalis had joined the Indians and were fighting against us. Pappa was clearly worried; he felt the circumstances were different this time, and the war had come to Adamjee Nagar. He felt if we went to Dacca, we would live under the protection of our army in the cantonment until the war was over.

So, the whole family climbed into our navy blue Fiat 1100, along with whatever belongings we could fit. Ammi and Pappa sat in the front, and Khusro Bhaijan and Maliha Apa sat in the back with me. I loved sitting on the brown leather back seat of my car, letting the wind blow on my face, but Ammi told me to roll up the window glass tight. I complained that it was getting quite hot and muggy inside with all the things we had stuffed in our car, so Pappa opened the front quarter light glass window to let some air in.

I was worried about leaving Kabooter behind, but Pappa said there was no room for him in the car and that he would be fine anyway. As we left our house, he was sitting perched up on top of his pigeon house, staring at us.

We drove out of the Adamjee Nagar compound and took the road to Dacca. The usually bustling two-way road was almost deserted. The journey took less than an hour, but it seemed eternally long. Along the way, we saw small bands of Mukti Bahini patrolling on foot, in cycle rickshaws, and on tractors. They were mostly thin, young, and dark-skinned men wearing either lungis or very little clothing. Some carried rifles or automatic weapons, while others were armed with sticks and machetes.

Picture 15: A Mukti Bahini patrol

Both Ammi and Pappa looked visibly shaken, and Pappa was driving very fast. Ammi was flipping the beads of her Tasbeeh faster than Pappa was driving the car. She was loudly repeating verses from the Quran, begging Allah for divine intervention to save our family. Near Dacca, we saw Pakistani troops in heavily camouflaged trucks, and we breathed a sigh of relief. We were stopped at one of the army checkpoints, where they searched our car, made sure we spoke Urdu, and quickly let us in.

We arrived at Mr. Huq's house in the Dacca Cantonment that afternoon and hurriedly unloaded our car. This was a rather uninteresting, plain, two-story, square-looking box of a house with dirty, pale-white exterior walls. The small, fenced garden at the front of the house was in disarray; overgrown bushes and shrubs tangled wildly as if reflecting the turmoil in East Pakistan.

Mrs. Huq was a middle school teacher at the nearby junior cadet school. The school was closed and abandoned in those days, so she stayed home. She was a very kind lady who opened her door for us and cooked delicious food for everyone in the house. Three other Bihari families had taken shelter under her roof. Like us, these families were also Urdu-speaking immigrants from West Pakistan or India. We didn't know any of them, but in times of adversity, strangers came together very quickly, and we all became good friends. The house was overcrowded, but we felt comfortable being among people of our own kind.

Behind the house was a very large concrete area that, in better days, had been used for military parades. Just across the parade ground were the headquarters of Lt. General A. A. K. Niazi, commander in chief of the Pakistan Army in East Pakistan. A huge green-and-white Pakistani flag with a crescent moon and star fluttered proudly in front of the building. There was always a lot of hustle and bustle around the headquarters, and one could see army Jeeps and big, heavy motorcycles pulling in and out of the compound, which was heavily guarded by Military Police. I would sometimes see General Niazi and his secretary arriving at his office in a black Mercedes.

Pappa believed we would be safer in the cantonment, but he could not have been more wrong. Dacca Cantonment was the worst place to be in during the war. The Pakistan Army was no match for the superior might of the Indian Army, and it soon became very clear that the cantonment area was the Indian Air Force's prime target. There was constant aerial bombardment of the cantonment. Every day, we would count ten to twelve sorties coming in to bombard the cantonment area. Pappa said it was like we had come 'out of the frying pan and into the fire'. This was the first time I had heard that phrase.

6
The Fall of Dacca

This was a war that was lost before it even started. By December 1971, almost every Bengali had turned against the West Pakistanis, whom they considered to be foreign invaders. The masses had revolted, and there were student uprisings in all the colleges and universities across East Pakistan. Common people took up arms to drive the non-Bengalis from their land. The West Pakistani government was completely paralyzed.

Numerous battalions of the East Bengal Regiment and the East Pakistan Rifles, once belonging to the Pakistan Army, defected to India. They crossed the border and were now fighting alongside their old enemy to defeat the Pakistani troops. Under the supervision of the Indians, they organized camps inside Indian Territory to train guerilla fighters. With the help of the Indian Army, the fighters were organized into various divisions, and Bengal was geographically divided into eleven sectors; the Sector Commanders directed the guerrilla warfare in the struggle for independence from Pakistan.

The Bengali Army units, along with their civilian militia, now freely patrolled the countryside, and the Pakistan Army was confined to bigger cities and military cantonments. It was quite clear that East Pakistan had slipped out of the hands of the West Pakistanis.

During the thirteen-day war, the Bengali renegade army units attacked East Pakistan from the Indian side of the border. The Bengali militia and Mukti Bahini fought a guerilla war against the Pakistan Army, and even ordinary citizens aided the Indian Army in the fight for their liberation from Pakistan. It was a one-sided war.

During the initial days of the war, we could see Pakistani Sabre fighter jets chasing the Indian MiG and Hunter aircraft. We even watched some dogfights in the skies, and I remember seeing a Pakistani Sabre jet engulfed in a ball of fire before it crashed into a huge plume of smoke. As the days went by, there were fewer and fewer Pakistani aircraft in the air, and the Indian Air Force took full command of the skies. By the eighth of December, the Pakistani Air Force's Tejgaon Airfield in Dacca was destroyed by heavy enemy bombardment, completely grounding all Pakistani aircraft. We felt scared and defenseless. Our only remaining protection was the Light Antiaircraft (Ack-Ack) Battery in Dacca Cantonment. The anti-aircraft guns defended the cantonment valiantly for the next few days, but, ultimately, they were no match for the Indian Army's superior air power.

Soon, the antiaircraft gunfire died down as well, and all we heard were the Indian bombers flying unchallenged in the skies. It seemed like the Indian Air Force had complete command of the airspace. Dacca Cantonment was their prime target, and they used a carpet-bombing strategy to subdue our army. Some days, the bombs would fall around us all day long. Sometimes, the bombs would fall so close to us that we could hear the hissing noise created by the friction of the falling arsenal. But what scared me most was the loud boom and shockwave caused by supersonic aircraft as they sped through the vast sky above. I learned that was the sound made by fighter jets when they travel faster than the speed of sound and break the sound barrier.

During the bombardments, we would hide under the staircase in the middle of Mr. Huq's house. My brother, sister, and I would huddle close to Ammi and Pappa until the all-clear sirens were sounded. Every four to six hours, we would hear the warning air raid sirens and then the usual sounds of Indian Air Force MiG aircraft, followed by explosions. It became a painfully familiar routine. The bombs were dropping everywhere, causing loud explosions. The windows would shake, and the whole house trembled, but, by some miracle, we survived.

After the raids, children would go out to see the craters caused by the bombs. Some were really large, and once, we found a small crater with an unexploded napalm bomb very close to our house. We would play in the yard until the warning sirens sounded again, and then we would rush back to the house and hide under the staircase.

In between the air raids, the grown-ups would gather in Mr. Huq's living room and talk. They would sit on the sofas while the children sat on the checkered carpet. Mrs. Huq would serve tea and sometimes cookies, too. The conversation would always gravitate toward our current predicament.

"I hope this war comes to an end soon," Mr. Huq would say in his usual deep, melancholic voice.

"Such a waste of precious life and property. And the children have missed so much schooling," Ammi agreed as she sat down on a sofa.

"This is such a bigger mess than the 1965 war. Much bigger! This time, the enemy is within us. The Bengalis are no longer with us," Mr. Huq replied.

"Well, you can't blame the Bengalis. We are in this mess because our army won't accept the people's decision," Pappa said. "I wish they had let Mujibur Rahman form the government when he won the elections!"

"Yes! He did win the elections fair and square," said Mr. Huq.

"It's not that simple, brother!" Mr. Rauf interjected. "This is not something that happened overnight." Mr. Rauf, who had also taken shelter in this house, always seemed to have the most intelligent comments. He was a fair, handsome young man and appeared quite learned.

"What you see today is the natural result of hate that has been spread over the last two decades." He continued, "Our West Pakistani brothers have suppressed the Bengalis for years, and now the Bengalis are retaliating. There is too much hate now."

Pappa agreed, "Yeah, hate is a powerful motivator; it has made the Bengalis blind to reasoning."

"Of course, hate spreads like wildfire. See how quickly things have spiraled down in front of our eyes?" Mr. Huq uttered, looking very miserable.

"You could say the Pakistani Army was just protecting the sovereignty of our country and, therefore, had the right to suppress the anarchy. But enough is enough." Mr. Rauf threw up his arms in the air. "How could they justify governing East Pakistan when the entire nation wants us out? What should have happened is that they should have held a referendum and just let the people decide if they wanted to go separate or not."

"That is so right, Rauf." Mr. Huq lamented. "You see, the Indians did not help either. They did not like a united Pakistan, and all these years, they have been adding fuel to the fire by aiding and emboldening the Bengali separatists." "But why doesn't anyone ever talk about all the sacrifices we, the Biharis and West Pakistanis, have made for Bengal?" Pappa was frustrated yet helpless. "There was nothing in East Bengal before partition, and we have worked hard with our sweat and blood, shoulder to shoulder with the Bengalis, to make this land what it is today."

No one answered. There was complete silence in the room, as if the air raid sirens had just sounded.

At eight, my mind could hardly comprehend what was being said, but I would still sit down and listen quietly, just like my brother and sister did. The men would talk about our situation and the possible outcomes of our ordeal for long periods of time since there wasn't anything else for them to do. We would sit around and talk for hours until the sirens sounded again.

One day, the sirens sounded as usual, and we hid under the staircase. We heard the Indian aircraft swoop down low, and a few anti-aircraft guns crackled, but no loud explosions followed. We were perplexed and somewhat curious. When the all-clear sirens sounded, we went outside and were surprised to see thousands of pink-and-orange pamphlets falling from the sky. They fluttered and descended toward us like a big swarm of birds and fell all around us. All the children had fun trying to catch them. These flyers were sent by the Indian General, Sam Manekshaw, and told our troops that they were surrounded and must surrender immediately. The pamphlets seemed to have a very sobering effect on the grownups, who suddenly seemed even more distressed.

At night, there was a blackout, during which no one was allowed to turn on any lights. The blackout was enforced by the Pakistan Army to collectively minimize outdoor light in the cantonment. It was thought, at that time, that any lights would give away our location to enemy aircraft and invite targeted bombing of our neighborhoods. So, we didn't turn on any lights after sunset. It was pitch black during the nights and very scary.

We had heard that Bengali people were throwing flashlights on our glass windows at night to try to identify Bihari homes for targeted bombings by the Indians. So, we covered the glass windows of Mr. Huq's house from the outside with sheets of black paper. When we ran out of black paper, we simply put old newspapers on the glass to prevent reflection. Mr. Rauf said it was a crazy notion and did not make sense, but we did it anyway since the adults felt we didn't have anything to lose.

It was rumored, in those days, that the Seventh Fleet of the US Navy would come to Pakistan's aid. Pakistan was an ally of the United States during the Cold War years, while India was in the Soviet bloc. The US Navy hurriedly commissioned a special task force as a show of force in support of Pakistan. The Task Force 74 was put together from the Seventh Fleet off South Vietnam and consisted of the USS Enterprise and nine support ships. It was dispatched to the Bay of Bengal on 8 December, five days after the start of the war. However, a Soviet naval fleet from Vladivostok intercepted US Task Force 74 in a potentially deadly Cold War standoff that could have easily triggered World War III. As it was, the small Task Force 74 was in no position to affect the outcome of the war, and it was felt to be an act of political maneuvering by Henry Kissinger and Richard Nixon. The United States was already heavily involved in the Vietnam War at that time and was not interested in another conflict that could potentially lead to World War III.

But even if the US had attacked and the aircraft carrier had seized air superiority over East Pakistan, they could not have reversed the outcome of the military campaign the Pakistan Army was rapidly losing on the ground. Yet, against all odds, the families sheltering in Mr. Huq's house continued to foolishly hope that the USS Enterprise would somehow save us. Though, deep down, I think we knew well that such an outcome was impossible and that the end was near.

We also knew that the Pakistan Army was profoundly overstretched. They were engaged heavily on the Western front, meaning there was no hope of further reinforcements from West Pakistan. We knew there was no help coming for us.

Trapped inside our house in the cantonment, we were completely cut off from the outside world. Telephone lines were down, and we had neither newspaper nor television. Our only source of news was the large radiogram in Mr. Huq's study. Radio Pakistan was still functional and broadcasting fake reports of Pakistani victories on all fronts, but Akashvani Radio broadcasts from across the border in India were presenting a different and frightening picture. Akashvani All India Radio, along with the Free Bengal Radio Centre, was a propaganda tool used by the Bangladeshi government in exile to boost the morale of the Bengali freedom fighters as well as for psychological warfare against the Biharis.

Fortunately, news from the BBC and Voice of America was less biased. These radio channels accurately reported the situation on the ground, and the situation did not look good for us. A week into the war, we heard that the Indians had captured Jessore and Sylhet and that the Indian Army, aided by the Mukti Bahini, was advancing toward Dacca. A day later, Mymensingh,

Kushtia, and Noakhali also fell into Indian control. The enemy was rapidly gaining the upper hand.

With the fall of Dacca now imminent, mass panic broke out in the Dacca Cantonment. It was a helpless and sinking feeling. We felt very isolated and scared. We knew there was no help coming and that the enemy was clearly winning the war. We did not know how the victorious Indians would treat civilians. We feared for our lives.

In those days of utter chaos, a handful of people were able to take refuge in the Hotel Intercontinental in Dacca. Another small group of Bihari women and children was able to board the few remaining single-propeller aircraft and fly out of Dacca. We watched a few helicopters, as well as single-engine Beaver and Twin Otter aircraft, take off from the grounds behind our house to evacuate some women and children to Burma. My six-year-old friend, Naeem, was on one of these helicopters with his older brother and infant sister. Ready to fly out of Dacca, he jumped from the chopper into the arms of his mother, who was staying behind. He was too scared to be separated from her. His siblings escaped in the chopper to Burma along with a small group of Urdu-speaking women and children. There were only a handful of people who escaped Dacca in those final days, but for the majority of Biharis in East Pakistan, defeat and even death seemed inevitable.

We had spent seven terrible days in Mr. Huq's house when the grownups decided it was too dangerous to stay in the cantonment due to the constant bombardment. They realized that the enemy was at our doorstep and ready for the final assault. We also heard that the Pakistan Army units were retreating and regrouping inside the Dacca Bowl for their last stand. It was clear that when the Indian Army launched its final attack on Dacca Cantonment, there would be intense door-to-door fighting resulting in mass casualties. We needed to escape.

My parents faced a tough decision, though. They knew they had to escape the cantonment, but they had no idea where to go. Mr. Rauf once again came up with the best answer. He was an electrical engineer at a powerplant just outside Dacca, and his house was located near the new airport, which was still under construction. He had moved his family to West Pakistan before the start of hostilities, and he offered to take us to his now vacant house in the outskirts of Dacca. Pappa felt we would be safer there.

So, during a lull in the airstrikes, we all got in our cars, and a small convoy of four cars left the cantonment. I remember we had an Opel Kadett, a Volkswagen Bus, and our 1967 Fiat 1100, but I don't remember the fourth car. Before the journey began, we painted the upper halves of all our headlights black due to blackout curfew regulations.

We reached Mr. Rauf's house late in the evening and unloaded. It was a modern-looking concrete house with straight, clean lines and minimal decor. This was a relatively new neighborhood just off the main highway and quite sparsely populated. Many of the houses, as well as the airport, were still under construction. Rows of bland houses and barren lots gave the neighborhood the appearance of a ghost town.

We had brought enough food and supplies to last us the next few days. It was quite peaceful in this new place. There were no more of the constant sirens, the sounds of aircraft, anti-aircraft guns, or loud bombs. What a contrast to the last few days in the cantonment! We felt relieved.

But the end really had come. The main line of defense of the Pakistan Armed Forces, surrounded by India in the east, west, and north, had collapsed under the weight of the Indian Army's fierce onslaughts. Battered and disjointed, the remnants of the once-proud Pakistan Army tried to form small pockets of resistance but proved unable to hold back the waves upon waves of Indian armored divisions. With no substantial resistance along the entire length of the front, the Indian armored divisions, infantrymen, and supply vehicles swept through the marshy Bangladeshi countryside to secure the prime objective of the thirteen-day war: the capital city of Dacca. Major General Jack Jacob of the Indian Eastern Command led the charge into Dacca.

The Indians, thus poised for the final victorious dash that, by its sheer momentum, would take them to Dacca, hope began to dwindle in the Pakistani camp. Hopelessly short of men and supplies, the Commander in Chief of the Eastern Front of the Pakistan Army, Lt. General Amir Abdullah Khan Niazi, surrendered on the afternoon of 16 December 1971. The surrender ceremony took place in the jam-packed Ramna Racecourse stadium, very close to the house we had left just two days ago. The surrender documents were signed between Lt. Gen. AAK Niazi and the commander in chief of the Eastern Sector of the Indian Army, Lt. General Jagjit Singh Arora.

Picture 16: Gen Arora and Gen Niazi signing the surrender document.

The surrender was a highly publicized event, and as a Bengali crowd cheered, officers of the Pakistan Army ceremonially lay down their arms. The photograph of the official surrender ceremony and the two generals signing the surrender document made headlines across the world, and the event is considered to be one of the largest surrenders of armed troops in history.

The quick fall of Dacca was one of the greatest debacles in military history, and even the Mukti Bahini and their Indian allies had not expected such a swift victory. The thirteen-day war was one of the shortest in modern times, and Lt. General AAK Niazi was heavily criticized for surrendering such a large army so quickly and without putting up a fight. But many also commended him for preventing further bloodshed. Really, a fight would have only prolonged the inevitable. His quick surrender probably saved hundreds of thousands of lives on both sides.

7
A Narrow Escape

Elated with the triumph of the Indian Army, the Mukti Bahini moved in for the kill. They dragged Bihari and Pakistani men from their homes and murdered them in front of their families. They looted houses and set fire to entire neighborhoods. Women were raped, and children were killed. There was murder and mayhem all over East Pakistan. The once idyllic Bangladeshi countryside became a bloodbath.

One such group of miscreants found their way into the neighborhood where my family had taken refuge. Having no illusion about this group's intentions, the grownups set quickly to work. Curtains were drawn, lights were extinguished, and doors were locked from the outside to give the house a deserted look – a ridiculous and unrealistic hope that the Mukti Bahini might pass us by, assuming the house to be uninhabited.

Next, all the doors and windows were bolted from the inside and barricaded with heavy furniture. After securing all the entrances that led into the house, we raced to the second floor and locked ourselves in the bedroom. Again, the door was secured, and we huddled close to each other, waiting for destiny to make its next move. This time, we had no adult men in the room with us. The women had locked them up in the bathroom to hide them since the Mukti Bahini was specifically targeting Bihari men. I was really scared. Ammi grabbed my hand and pulled me closer to her.

From a slit between the curtains, we had a clear view of the remnants of the once-upscale neighborhood. The waning crescent moon barely cast any light on the surroundings, but a few streetlamps and burning houses gave some clue to the movements of the Mukti Bahini in the nearby lanes. Most of the houses appeared abandoned or vacant. Some houses had no walls or roofs, either because they were still under construction or they'd been destroyed by the recent bombings.

In the street next to ours, smoke billowed from a few houses. A band of young zealots from the Mukti Bahini moved into our street. Between life and death, there hung a frail curtain of seven houses. In that desperate and lonely moment, we offered a silent prayer, placed our fate in God's hand, and waited.

We waited. And waited. An hour passed by. But nothing happened. It seemed the neighborhood was suddenly quiet again. The sporadic gunfire had died down as well. It seemed that, somehow, our prayers had been answered and the Mukti Bahini had left us. It was eerily quiet, and the silence was unbearable; we did not know what to make of it. We spent the night fearing for the worst. Later, we found out that the 16th Infantry Division of the Pakistan Army was retreating to Dacca from Bogra and Nator through the same area that night. Sensing the presence of a mighty army division close by, the Mukti Bahini had dispersed quickly. We, thus, escaped one of the most terrifying encounters of our lives on the first night of surrender.

It was the morning of 17 December that we heard a distant rumble. It was a strange and ever-growing noise, unlike anything I had ever heard before. It seemed to be coming from the west side of the house, from behind the fields. I ran up to the second floor and peered from the bathroom glass awning window. I could see lush green rice fields as far as my eyes could see. Today, the green shoots of the rice fields were waving and undulating with the breeze, even more so than usual. Soon, I could make out rhythmically marching men among the rolling green fields in the distance. Then, I saw wave upon wave of Indian infantrymen clothed from head to toe in green uniforms moving toward us. The rice fields dancing in synchrony with the marching columns of infantrymen created a surreal image that I still remember vividly to this day. Behind the troops came hundreds of Indian T-55 tanks, filling the air with that loud rumbling noise.

We were jubilant to see the Indian Army advancing towards Dacca, and we congratulated each other. The adults told us that the Indian Army would act according to proper rules of engagement, unlike the rogue Mukti Bahini, who were merely a gang of thugs bent on killing Biharis. It felt strange to be welcoming the Indian Army, our sworn enemy, to take over our city. But these Indian troops were to be our saviors now. They would save us from the Mukti Bahini, who were slaughtering us. We were quite sure that with the Indian

Army in town, there would be some law and order in a city that had seen none in the last few weeks.

The Indian Army did take control of the situation very quickly. They established zonal command centers and appointed area commanders. The perimeter of Dacca was secured. A curfew was imposed. The Pakistan Army was quickly disarmed. The Mukti Bahini was also brought under control, to the extent that was possible. The violent revenge of the Mukti Bahini was restrained somewhat, though it still carried on in small pockets outside Dacca.

8
Back at the Cantonment

The next day, we heard that sanctuary zones were being created throughout Bangladesh. Any Bihari entering a sanctuary zone would be placed under the protection of the Indian Army and would then be safely escorted back to West Pakistan. One of the sanctuary zones was the same Dacca Cantonment from which we had escaped just a few days ago.

Pappa was determined to get us to the sanctuary zone. He went out to look for help, and an hour later came back with good news. He had flagged down a convoy of the Indian Army and told them about his plight. They took pity and sent two sepoys of the Indian Army with him. These men would help us get to the cantonment, but we needed to leave immediately. We were only allowed to take a few clothes and essential items, and we had to leave our car behind. Pappa thought it would be a kind gesture to leave the keys in the ignition so a Bengali could use our abandoned car. My brother, who was twelve at the time, objected and wanted to throw the keys in the nearby pond, but Pappa said it would be better if someone could benefit from our loss and use the car. We got into the two army Jeeps and headed for the Dacca Cantonment.

On the way, we saw devastation everywhere. We saw torched neighborhoods, collapsed houses, and large craters formed by the bombs that had been dropped from the air. We saw smoke rising in serpentine columns from the ruins of the new airport. We passed large crowds of jubilant Bengalis celebrating on the streets. They were chanting, "Joy Bangla! Joy Bangla!"

For the first time, we saw the green and red flag of Bangladesh flying over houses and buildings.

Fortunately, when we arrived back at the cantonment, Mr. Huq's house was still intact and locked. We quickly unlocked the house and went inside. A sixth family with two little children joined us this time. The house was overcrowded beyond capacity, but it was quite comforting to be back in familiar surroundings. We gave a collective sigh of relief.

The scene in the cantonment, however, was chaotic. Thousands of Pakistani soldiers were aimlessly roaming around the cantonment. They still wore their khaki uniform, but their outfits were unironed and crumpled. They no longer carried any heavy arms but were allowed to keep small arms for personal protection. It looked like they had plenty of time on their hands, and they would just hang around in small groups, doing nothing but chatting, smoking, or playing cards. They had the dejected look of a defeated army and looked confused. It seemed that they didn't know what was going on either.

We could see a flurry of activity at Lt. General Niazi's headquarters. We saw a lot of Indian troops going in and out of the building, and there was a lot of hustle and bustle. Jeeps and military police motorcycles were pulling in and out of the compound. The large Pakistani flag in front of the building had been taken down, and the Indian flag flew side by side with the solid green and red flag of the nascent nation. Green representing the lush landscape and the red circle in the middle representing blood of the Bengalis shed during the Liberation War.

Many houses in the cantonment, as well as army barracks and schools, had been evacuated to make room for the incoming troops and Bihari refugees. Furniture was removed from classrooms and piled up behind the school building to make room for the swarm of incoming refugees. Those who could not be accommodated inside the buildings were housed in thousands of specially erected tents. Soon, the entire cantonment grounds became a large makeshift camp. While most of the people lived in these makeshift accommodations, we were fortunate to be able to stay in Mr. Huq's house. Though the house provided shelter and comfort, it was overcrowded, and we had no electricity.

We quickly ran out of food as well, but the Pakistan Army had set up kitchens that provided three meals a day. I would go with my father and Khusro Bhaijan to these large kitchens and wait in line for hours to get food. However, after such a long wait, the rewards were quite sweet, and I remember bringing home sooji ka halwa and puri for breakfast.

One morning, as I was walking back from the kitchen, I decided to make my journey more exciting by taking a detour. Rather than walking on the sidewalk, I took the muddied path behind the school. I decided to climb on the heap of chairs and desks that were taken out of the school to make room for refugees. I meandered through the piles of furniture stacked against the red brick wall. From the corner of my eye, I spotted something gold and shiny underneath a wooden desk by the school wall. In my curiosity, I hurried to pick it up. It was a circular golden medal with a crescent and star at its center, suspended from a golden bar with a short striped red and green ribbon. A Hilal-e-Jurrat medallion was shining in all its glory. Its beautiful gold engravings and brilliant shine mesmerized me, and I quickly hid it in my pocket. It probably belonged to a Pakistani soldier who had been awarded this honor for gallantly fighting the Indians in the Indo-Pakistani War of 1965. No doubt, fearing repercussions from the now victorious Indian Army, he'd probably hidden it here, where no one was likely to find it.

I kept the medallion hidden in my pocket for two days and looked at it in awe when no one was around. This was my little secret, which I kept from everyone. At the same time, I felt guilty for 'stealing' this beautiful medallion from a brave soldier of the Pakistani Army. After a couple of days, fear overtook me. What if the Indians arrested me for possessing this medallion that symbolized courageous attacks against them? I dug a little hole in the ground and buried the medallion. My little secret stayed with me forever.

Behind Lt. General Niazi's headquarters, there was a huge pile of disabled munitions. The Pakistani Army was dumping all their ammunition in this area. There were mortars, grenades, rifles, and machine guns; all sorts of weapons and unused bullets were strewn across the grounds. We would walk around these grounds and come across some of the most colorful bullet jackets. I was so fascinated by the colorful stripes around the waists of these silver or chrome bullets that I started collecting the bullets as trophies. I accumulated quite a good-sized collection, and my friends and I started playing with these colorful bullets. We became used to so many different types of munitions, and after a while, all of us children could identify the different types of grenades, machine guns, Tommy guns, and Sten guns.

Small bands of weary and dejected Pakistani soldiers arrived in the Dacca Cantonment every day. Some came in on small convoys of Jeeps and trucks, while others simply came on foot. Once they arrived, they would throw their weapons into the huge pile of munitions and report to the big white tent that had been erected by the Indian Army. Here, they would get an identification number and some sort of registration. Then, they would either erect their own tents or find accommodation inside one of the buildings.

Over the next few days, we started seeing more and more soldiers from the Indian Army in the cantonment. They looked just like our soldiers, except for the green khaki uniforms they wore. They would mostly be seen driving around in their WWII-era Jeeps. We came to recognize them by their distinctive dress codes. Soldiers from the Maratha Regiment wore the most colorful paraphernalia, while the Gurkhas wore slouched hats that drooped down one side of their heads. The Rajputs wore flat brown helmets and thick handlebar mustaches. And for the first time, we saw some Sikh soldiers who had beards and very long hair tied in a knot on their heads, and they wore neatly pleated turbans.

9
Refugees in Our Own Homeland

Each day, we saw hundreds of Bihari civilians arriving at the Dacca Cantonment refugee camp. They had walked miles, sometimes barefoot, carrying whatever possessions they had to reach the safety of the UN-supervised refugee camp. Some even carried their sick and elderly relatives on their backs. They told us horror stories of the brutal killings and atrocities committed by the Mukti Bahini. We heard of entire families murdered and women raped, and even teenagers had been killed in cold blood. We learned that the situation in the smaller cities around Dacca was grim, and now the Bengalis were killing Biharis with the same vengeful ferocity as the West Pakistanis had done just a few weeks earlier. A full-scale counter-genocide was unfolding. We thanked God that we were in the cantonment and under the protection of the Indian Army.

Most of these incoming refugees had immigrated to East Pakistan from the Bihar Province of India. Some were originally from other parts of India, like my family. Others were from West Pakistan. But we were all lumped together as Biharis (people from Bihar) to separate us from the indigenous people (the Bengalis). The common denominator was that the Biharis did not speak the Bengali language; they mostly spoke Urdu, and even though they shared the same religion as the Bengalis, their culture was somewhat different. These Bihari Muslims supported the Pakistani government during the civil war and wanted to remain in a united Pakistan. Most of these people had come here in search of a better life after the 1947 partition of India, but some had been living in East Pakistan for generations. They had made East Pakistan their home. They owned land and businesses. But now, East Pakistan was not theirs anymore, and they were not welcome in their own homeland.

Within days, a sprawling city of tents took shape in front of our eyes. Neatly lined rows of white tents popped up in the grounds between our house and Lt. General Niazi's command office. As the days passed, the number of incoming refugees swelled, and soon, an entire tent city came to life. By some estimates, the Dacca Cantonment camp was home to almost 25,000 refugees in the days after the fall.

One day, while playing between tents, I suddenly came across my old friend, Fayaz. He and I had gone to school together, and his mother, Mrs. Khatoon, had been my Montessori teacher at the Narayanganj Preparatory English School. We were jubilant to see each other after two months, and we hugged and played for a long time. His family had arrived at the camp a couple of days ago, but, unfortunately, his older brother had been killed a few days earlier by the Mukti Bahini. While my parents were very happy to see familiar faces, the meeting between our two families was quite somber.

Interestingly, the same day as I ran into Fayaz, Pappa encountered a long-lost friend, too, in Major Venkataraman. Though my father was Muslim and Major Venkataraman was Hindu, they had been close childhood friends. They went to high school and college together, and both were good soccer players. They had played for the Osmania University football team in Hyderabad, India. After graduating from college, Pappa left for East Pakistan, while Major Venkataraman joined the Indian Army. Now, he had come to Dacca as a major in the victorious Indian Army. The two men shook hands hesitantly in front of on-looking soldiers, and then the major took my father into his makeshift office, where the two drank tea and spoke of old times. The major was very kind and empathized with my father's situation.

When Pappa came back, he told us the major had offered to help search for Pappa's cousins, who also lived in Adamjee Nagar. He also offered to take Ammi back to our old home in Adamjee Nagar to see if any important items or documents could be salvaged. The major said it would be too dangerous for my father to go due to the unrest and violence that specifically targeted Bihari men, so, instead, my mother could go under the protection of the Indian Army.

The next morning, two Indian soldiers arrived in a Jeep to pick up Ammi. "Major Venkataraman sent us," said one of them sternly.

Ammi was ready. My friend Fayaz's mother, Mrs. Khatoon, who had taught in the same school as Ammi, had volunteered to accompany her on this journey. The two women climbed on the back of the Jeep, and the soldiers took the front seats. As I saw the Jeep speed away from our house, I had a gut-wrenching empty feeling inside me. What if she doesn't come back? Pappa threw a comforting arm around me but didn't say anything. We stood there for a while, staring at the empty road long after the Jeep had disappeared in the distance.

They left around ten in the morning and didn't return until seven at night. It was a long few hours. When Ammi came back, she had tears in her eyes. She brought with her some important documents, including my father's diplomas, pension, and insurance policies. She said that our home in Adamjee Nagar had been completely ransacked and destroyed. The curtains had been torn down and the windows shattered, and furniture had been thrown out, and all precious items had been looted. She was able to salvage some of the important papers and family pictures that had been strewn across the floor. She also visited the homes of our extended family, who resided in Adamjee Nagar, but their houses were abandoned, and no one knew where the occupants had gone.

Ammi told me she did not see Kabooter when she went to our house. He would usually be in his pigeon birdhouse or perched atop the sunroom roof, but Ammi did not find him there. She said the coop door was ajar, and the chickens had also gone away. I wondered if Kabooter and my chickens had all become refugees, too.

During the short trip, Ammi also witnessed a large number of Bihari mill workers stranded inside the Adamjee Jute Mills compound. The mills had been shut down just before the onset of the war, and workers and their families had now taken refuge inside the mill sheds. According to some reports, as many as twenty thousand Biharis from Adamjee Nagar and the surrounding communities had taken shelter within the compound, living virtually under siege. The mills were surrounded by vengeful Bengalis, who threatened to attack at any time. Just around 10 a.m. on 16 December, the Mukti Bahini started shelling the compound. Fearing an imminent massacre, the Indian Army quickly deployed a platoon of just fifty or so soldiers to protect these Biharis, and the situation was tense. Without resistance, the Biharis inside the mills hoisted white flags to plead for surrender and ceasefire. They had no electricity or running water, and living conditions inside the compound were deplorable. We learned, too, that food and essential supplies were running short in the Adamjee Nagar refugee camp, and those few who ventured beyond the walls in search of food were butchered mercilessly by the Bengali militia.

Every day, we heard more and more terrifying stories from the new arrivals at the Dacca refugee camp. We heard of murder and ethnic cleansing of Biharis in Dinajpur, Thakurgaon, Meymensigh, and Brahmanbaria. In Dacca, the situation was a little better, and the Bihar Regiment prevented an imminent bloodshed in Mohammadpur, a predominantly Bihari neighborhood. But even here, there was lawlessness and mayhem for many days. Just outside the cantonment, a group of young Bihari men were beaten and tortured for thirty minutes in front of a large crowd of jeering Bengalis before being slowly bayoneted to death. Thousands of Biharis and even Bengali supporters of United Pakistan were killed as the Mukti Bahini sought revenge for the atrocities committed by the Pakistanis. In many cases, the victims were tortured before being killed.

But amidst these horrific tales of savagery, there were also stories of friendship, compassion, and bravery that transcended culture and religion. My friend, Arif Iqbal, was a ninth grader at the Faujdarhat Cadet College near Chittagong. When his boarding school shut down without any notice, he had to leave immediately in the middle of the night. During the train journey from Faujdarhat to his home in Dacca, his Bengali friends shielded him from the Mukti Bahini, who searched the train compartment at the Comilla Railway Station. His teenage friends formed a human circle around him so the Mukti Bahini would not recognize him as a Bihari.

When the Mukti Bahini went on a killing rampage after the fall of Dacca, my friend Ras Siddiqui's father, who worked in the Central Public Works Department (PWD) Electricity, found refuge in the home of his Bengali co-worker. The Bengali engineer hid him for two days in his house before delivering him to the refugee camp in his Jeep; such were the tales that helped keep our faith in humanity during those terrible days following the fall of Dacca.

The next few days in the cantonment were surprisingly calm. We saw more people from the Red Cross and the United Nations High Commissioner for Refugees who started setting up field offices. They started registering the refugees so they could be located and tracked. They dispensed essential supplies and distributed food, warm clothing, sanitary products, and emergency supplies to all the civilian refugees.

The war had uprooted hundreds of thousands of people, and now these Biharis were strangers in the land in which they had lived for generations. No one knew what our fate would be. For the time being, we were safe within the sanctuary of the refugee camp but could not venture outside. We knew we would be killed if we were to leave the safety of the cantonment. We were refugees in our own homeland.

The Indians found themselves in a peculiar situation, too. They had invaded East Pakistan to crush and defeat the Pakistan Armed Forces. But now that the Pakistanis had surrendered, the Indians were obligated to protect their former adversaries under the Geneva Convention, which stipulates the humanitarian treatment of military and civilian prisoners of war. They had waged war against the Pakistani forces just a few days ago, and now they were supposed to safeguard these very enemy combatants.

Protecting the 54,000 or so army personnel was, perhaps, the easier task. More difficult was the task of protecting the two million Urdu-speaking Biharis, who were presumed to have collaborated with the Pakistan Army and now faced revenge at the hands of Bengalis. These Biharis were now the target of angry Bengali mobs. The Bihari neighborhoods across towns and cities in Bangladesh were cordoned off and surrounded by Mukti Bahini. Inside these neighborhoods, the stranded Bihari Muslims lived in fear for their lives. White flags dotted these streets in desperate pleas for mercy. The situation was very tense, especially in Chittagong, Sylhet, Gazipur, Mymensingh, Rajshahi, Comilla, Jessore, and Kushtia.

To their credit, the Indians tried their best to prevent further bloodshed. They deployed small army units all across the country to stop the Bengalis from storming Bihari neighborhoods and slaughtering the Urdu-speaking residents. The Indians knew that if they abandoned them, the Biharis would be killed in masses, and fearing international condemnation, they felt obligated to protect us, at least for the time being. And so, by a twist of fate, our enemy became our savior and protector.

Now that we were safe enough, under the protection of the Indian Army, and out of the reach of the Mukti Bahini, Pappa intensified his efforts to find his cousin. One day, Pappa came back with a UN aid worker. This German man told us in broken English that his team had tried to locate our relatives in Dacca and Adamjee Nagar but had been unsuccessful.

"Mr. Qumar'uddin! Ve could not find your relatiffe. Maybe zey already go to Pakistan."

He told us that he had checked the names of refugees in the Adamjee Nagar Refugee Camp as well as some other camps in Dacca, but he also told us that lists are being updated every day as new refugees are coming in, so we need not worry; it is possible they will show up soon to one of the sanctuary zones. The UN worker also told us that all civilian refugees would be separated from the military POWs and would be transferred outside the Dacca Cantonment area.

"Ve vill moffe you to houzing facility for ciffilians. Arh! Its fery kood, its fery zafe."

He rocked his hands up and down, trying hard to convince everyone that the new place will be 'very good and very safe'.

"I really don't know if we should go there," Ammi said. "I think we should stay with our army."

Pappa was skeptical. "I don't think we have a choice; we must do what they tell us."

"The military POWs are going to be returned to West Pakistan sooner or later, so we better stick with them." She feared if we were separated from the army, we might be left behind or, perhaps, worse.

"*Nein, nein*, ve vill look afder you und take care of you." The German man tried his best to reassure us in his broken accent.

Later that evening, the UN representative drove us in a truck to the Kilo Camp for refugees on the outskirts of Dacca. It was located close to the Cantt. Railway Station in the north of Dacca. Kilo Camp was set up in the newly constructed apartment buildings that were once supposed to house the families of Air Force personnel. The four-story apartments were not much more than rows of uninteresting, characterless gray concrete. There were no trees or greenery to speak of, and the area looked very bland. The apartments had never been inhabited and were unfurnished. We spent the next few days in a small, two-bedroom apartment on the second floor with the other families from Mr. Huq's house. The women and children slept on the floor in the bedrooms, while the men slept in the living room and corridors. There was no furniture in the rooms, so we sat and slept on the cement floors.

The Kilo Camp was a safe haven in the midst of chaos. As news of this safe haven spread, many Biharis from Dacca and surrounding areas started converging towards the camp. While some Biharis made a dash to Kilo Camp in their own cars, others hired trucks or buses and even private vehicles to get there. Sometimes, they defied hostile crowds on the road to get to Kilo Camp, and many paid exorbitant amounts of money to local Bengalis to guarantee safe passage. One day, I saw two busloads of refugees come into Kilo Camp.

Some refugees came with just clothes on their bodies, while others, with unrealistic expectations, brought furniture, fridges, television sets, and everything along. They had hoped to take all their belongings with them to West Pakistan.

Colonel Mohindarpal Singh 'Johar' of the Indian Army oversaw Kilo Camp, and he ordered a group of young men from among the refugees to start compiling a list of all the newcomers. These men sat under an open tent and made entries into a thick register. It was an extensive list that included their names, addresses, and number of family members. It included all their belongings and even the type and make of cars they had brought in.

Over the next few days, we had officials from the Red Cross and the United Nations High Commissioner for Refugees (UNHCR) visit us at the Kilo Camp. Each family was given rations, as well as a kerosene stove, an aluminum cooking pot, and cooking utensils. Our family of five got a sack of rice and lentils as well as a canister of ghee and cooking oil. I remember my family receiving an aluminum pot with a lid that stayed with us for the next many years. Since I was very young at that time, my family got a can of powdered milk, too.

We also got some warm clothing, sweaters, and cozy blankets. I remember receiving a blue-and-gray-checkered woolen Tartan blanket labeled 'Made in Scotland'. It was kind of rough and prickly, but it felt good in the winter weather. We also received some brown sweaters and warm woolen wraps that were taken from the now-defunct Pakistan Army storage depot.

During these days of confusion, no one knew exactly what to do or what would happen next. We knew that East Pakistan was no more and that we, Biharis, were not welcome in Bangladesh. But West Pakistan was far away. Essentially, we were stateless.

On Christmas Day, we learned that all the prisoners of war, including civilians, would be transported to West Pakistan, but no one knew when or how.

It was speculated that we would be taken to India by the Indian Army and, from there, conducted to Pakistan through the land route.

In preparation, the United Nations began to register us and gave us POW numbers. Civilians were also given CUPC (Civilians Under Protective Custody) numbers. Pappa was relieved that we had received the civilians under protective custody designation. He felt that the International Committee of the Red Cross was now responsible for our safety, and we should not come to harm.

Thousands of civilian refugees had been brought into the Kilo Camp. We were divided into several groups and instructed to stay together at all times.

10
The Long Journey Begins

It was rumored that refugees at Kilo Camp were going to be 'moved' on New Year's Eve. No one was sure where we would be moved to, but we were hopeful that we would finally be returned to Pakistan. Pakistan was more than a thousand miles away, which seemed quite far to be 'moved to'. Still, this was some progress, and there seemed to be a faint glimmer of hope in the air. After all, these were very uncertain times, and we seemed to have more speculation than answers.

As morning came, there was quite a bit of hustle and bustle in Kilo Camp. At dawn, we saw a long line of Indian Army trucks approaching our apartment complex in a two-lane formation. The big Ashok Leyland military trucks stopped right next to our building. The sound of idling engines reverberating back from the apartment walls was deafening. An Indian Army officer spoke to us on a horn loudspeaker and instructed us to come down from our apartments with our luggage. So, we brought down our belongings and lined up next to the trucks. The smell of the diesel fumes from the big trucks was nauseating, but at least the heat from the truck engines provided us with some welcome warmth in the cold December weather.

Then, very systematically, the Red Cross and Indian Army started loading us into the trucks. No one knew where we were going, but we were glad to be going somewhere. Maybe to Pakistan!

Our turn came late in the morning. We took our belongings and climbed into the back of the green military truck. It was a big open truck without any cover. We sat on the benches on either side while some people sat on the truck bed. We had a brown leather suitcase, a bistar bund, a woven wicker suitcase, and a small black metal suitcase – all our earthly belongings – and we hung on to them like heavenly possessions. We rode in the truck for two hours until we reached the river port of Narayanganj, very close to our own home in Adamjee Nagar.

We disembarked from the trucks and were instructed to walk over to the docks. It was very chaotic, and it seemed like thousands of people were coming from everywhere at once. There were lots and lots of people, but no one was making eye contact, and everyone seemed to be in their own world, like a bunch of scared zombies. The huge crowd of refugees was trying to get to the dockyard. We were all walking as fast as we could, and a few people stumbled and fell, too. Some people were old and infirm; some were young and energetic. There were a lot of women and children in the crowd. The refugees were carrying everything they possibly could bring with them. Some had suitcases or cane baskets. Others carried sacks, bags, buckets, cooking pots, everything imaginable. Some had simply tied their belongings into a cloth bundle, which they carried on their backs. Pappa was carrying the bistar bund and the brown leather suitcase. Khusro Bhaijan dragged the wicker cane basket and urged Maliha Apa to walk faster. Ammi was holding the metal suitcase with one hand and my sister's hand with the other. I was clinging to Pappa's shirt and running as fast as I could. I was afraid of getting lost in the crowd.

We assembled on the concrete floor of the dockyard. We could see large cranes, cargo, and warehouses all around us. Bales of jute, piled up three stories high, rose on either side of the dockyard. The Red Cross workers handed us pre-packed food boxes from the back of a truck, and we ate both breakfast and lunch together. It was Friday afternoon, so we prayed the Jumu'ah prayers on the dockyard. I stood next to my brother and father and offered Friday prayers.

An old steamboat was waiting for us at the dock. We all lined up in small groups, and the lengthy process of counting, registration, and recounting began. At last, the formalities were completed, and we boarded the paddle steamer in the late afternoon.

It was a large, flat-bottomed boat with small compartments on both the upper and lower decks and large open floor spaces with numerous long wood benches on the deck. Funnily, the steamer was called a 'Rocket' because, apparently, when it first started plowing the rivers of East Bengal in the 1920s, it was as fast as a rocket!

Picture 17: Rocket Boats

Though the old 'Rocket' steamer had a capacity of around six hundred or so passengers, nearly a thousand refugees were crammed onto its decks and cabins. By the time we got on the boat, most of the space was already occupied. My family found a covered area on the upper deck, under the smokestacks, and huddled together. It was very comforting to be close to my family. All five of us together.

Pappa opened the bistar bund and spread it out on the deck so we could sit on it. Ammi seemed tense; she grabbed my arm and said, "Don't you run around now; if you get lost, we will never find you." Her jaw clenched, and her grip tightened around my forearm.

I was scared myself; I promised Ammi I wouldn't move from that spot. "Where are they taking us?" Ammi asked after a while.

"Um, I don't know…" Pappa replied, staring blankly at the riverbank. "Can you ask someone?"

"There are so many people here, but I don't think anyone knows. And I don't think the Indian soldiers would talk to us," Pappa said tersely. "We better stay quiet and do whatever they tell us."

Just after sundown, the big paddlewheels of the steamboat started to turn. The steamer let out a bellowing horn and pulled away from the dock into the choppy waters. As the steamer started picking up speed, the wind took its cue and blew fiercely into our faces. It was very gusty, and sitting on the deck, we were completely exposed to the elements. Soon, night fell, and we were sailing down the River Meghna.

It was a stormy night. The steamer churned, listed, and groaned under the weight of its passengers. With every strong crosswind, the old steamer lurched dangerously. The moon was full, causing the tidal Meghna to toss the steamboat up and down on the currents. No one could sleep that night, and we feared that the overburdened ship would sink. It was a long and scary journey, and we didn't know where we were headed. I pushed closer into my mother's embrace and felt very safe. I finally fell asleep.

When I woke up the next morning, the steamer had come to port, and people were already disembarking. I held my mother's hand as we went down the wooden planks that formed makeshift stairs. A group of Pakistani soldier volunteers supervised the unloading and directed us toward the harbor building. The Indians had deployed some Pakistani units to help with the massive task of moving the refugees. These Pakistani soldiers wore plain khaki fatigues but didn't wear any hats nor carry any arms.

Next to the harbor building, the Pakistani Jawans had built a makeshift kitchen inside a large military tent. Here, they fried puris in large pans, which were filled to the brim with hot oil. The sight of puris simmering in boiling oil and the sweet aroma of freshly cooked bread was delightfully appetizing. I had not eaten since we were at the Narayanganj port, and it felt wonderful to get some warm food in my tummy. The puris were warm, sweet, and crispy, and, to me, puris had never tasted so good. After breakfast, we assembled next to the harbor building, and then we were organized into a long column and ordered to march.

After a short walk, we arrived at a rundown railway station. A rather derelict, stonewashed sign read Khulna, which we immediately recognized as a small station on the railway line between Bangladesh and India. We were exhausted but happy that we were at the railway station and boarding trains that would, hopefully, take us to Pakistan.

Outside the railway station, a group of hostile Bengalis had gathered to show their anger towards us. They looked emaciated and were scantily clad in lungi and banyan. There were some women in the group as well, who wore the traditional Bengali saris without any blouses, which left them almost bare-breasted. Some Bengalis started yelling at us and made threatening gestures, but we felt safe since we were protected by the Indian Army. The Indian Army made sure the protestors stayed far away from us and could not harm us. It was a strange feeling to know that our sworn Hindu 'enemies' were protecting us from our own, until recently Muslim compatriots.

The Khulna railway station looked completely desolate and abandoned. There were no trains or passengers on the platform, as the services were interrupted due to war. We walked past the empty platforms and were escorted to an open area just outside the railway station. A long train with red carriages, coupled together like an unyielding chain, waited for us. An old steam locomotive engine stood at the front of the carriages. The carriage windows were boarded with wood panels. We were told that this was for our protection so the angry Bengalis would not be able to throw stones through the windows. But Pappa said these were to prevent POWs from escaping the moving train.

We were asked to gather in a large open area between multiple railway tracks. We began the long and methodical task of boarding the train. Since there was no platform, we walked between tracks on wooden rail sleepers and pebbles and climbed up the ladder into the carriage. The Pakistani Jawans helped us once again, but this time to board the train. They hauled our luggage onto the train and helped the women and children climb the ladders into the carriage. We were counted and recounted before we got on board, and when we took our seats, we were counted again. More than one hundred civilians were boarded into carriages designed to hold sixty people. The carriage was quite crammed, and some people did not get seats.

Our railway carriage was a dismal gray, second-class railcar. It was dark and dull, and paint was erratically peeling off from dirty, pale white walls in many places. A row of ten low-back wooden benches facing each other were lined on one side of the aisle, while single-chair seats were located on the other side. Above each of the benches was a wooden sleeping berth. A sparse row of caged bulbs hung above the aisle that separated the benches from the single seats.

The Pakistani Jawans had prepared food for the journey, which they carried on their backs, and they brought four huge jute burlap bags into each compartment. The sacks were loaded with Namak pare and Shakar pare, salty and sugary cubes of deep-fried flatbread. This would be our food supply for the next few days. Then, six armed Indian soldiers took up position in a small chamber at the back of each carriage; two stood next to each of the two exits, and the heavy metal doors were locked.

11
A Never-Ending Train Ride

It was mid-afternoon when the old steam engine let out a loud and shrill whistle and slowly started to move. As it laboriously pulled out of the Khulna railyard and away from the crowd of jeering Bengalis, we breathed a sigh of relief. We thanked God that the train was moving and that we were finally on our way to Pakistan.

We peeked out of the window between the wooden panels and saw the rain-drenched, lush-green Bangladeshi countryside. We sat back and tried to take stock of our situation. Water along with Namak pare and Shakar pare were served for lunch. We ate the dried salty and sugary pare and washed them down with water.

Night fell, and we quietly ate more pare, drank more water, and went to sleep. We woke up in the morning, ate even more pare, drank even more water, and looked outside. The next day, we did the same, and the train kept moving. It was a monotonous routine, and we resigned ourselves to the confines of our small cabin. The train crossed the Bangladesh-India border at Darshana, and we passed through the sprawling city of Kolkata and its huge railway yard. We went over the very long Howrah Bridge over the Hooghly River and cut across West Bengal. We passed the stations of Gaya, Varanasi, Allahabad, Kanpur, and Bareilly, but still our journey continued. It seemed like a never-ending journey, but at least we knew that we were in Northern India and moving westward toward Pakistan.

From the boarded rail carriage windows, we could make out that some of these railway stations were big junctions of the Indian Railway. At Kolkata and Allahabad Junctions, we saw hundreds of trains pulling in and out of the station. The platforms were crammed with thousands of commuters, coolies, and food vendors selling chai, chat, kachoris, samosas, and boiled eggs. Even late in the night, these railway stations were full of people and brilliantly illuminated by thousands of light bulbs. The hustle and bustle of these stations was in stark contrast to the gloomy atmosphere inside our carriage.

The journey, which we thought would take only a couple of days, dragged on, and the train kept meandering from city to city. Soon, everyone became convinced that, just like the passengers, the train's engineer did not know where he was going either. Later, we found out that communications were terribly inefficient in those days and that the engineer would only learn that a city's POW camps were full after we had already arrived. Then, the train would move on to another city in search of a POW camp that could take us. We were tired, and no one knew where our next stop would be, but still, we were happy that our journey back home had at least started.

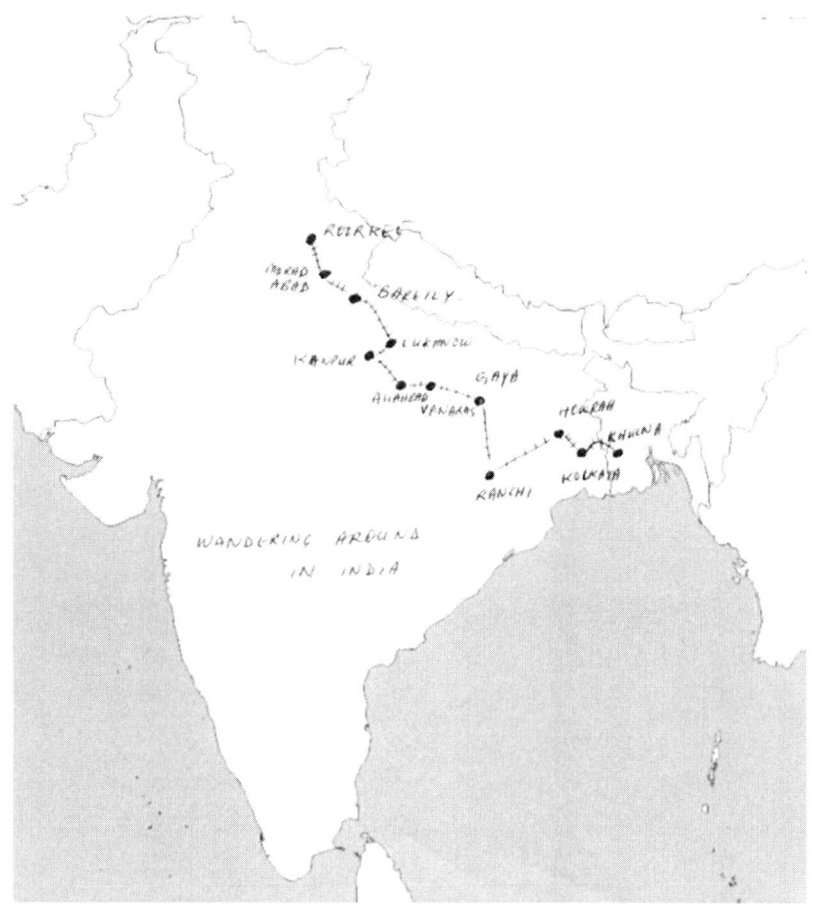

Figure 03: A never-ending train ride.

There was not much room in the carriage to move around. We sat on our wooden benches all day long and waited for our next meal. Some just stood in the aisle holding the leather strap hanging from the roof. The carriage was very stuffy due to the barricaded windows, and people stepped on each other's feet from overcrowding.

During the day, we tried to keep our spirits high by looking through the boarded windows at the gloomy countryside. Sometimes, while passing through uninhabited areas, the guards would allow us to open the glass panes to get fresh air.

At night, we sat under the dim light of caged bulbs hanging from the carriage roof and stared at the slowly oscillating ceiling fans. Since there was not enough space for everyone to lie down, we took turns sleeping on the cold and hard wooden benches. The grownups stayed up late, speculating on what would happen next or how and when they would get back home to Pakistan.

These were long and depressing days. Shut off from fresh air and sunlight and stuck inside the crammed compartments, some tried to pass the time by playing card games or matchstick puzzles. Some refugees speculated why the train was taking a zigzag course across northern India instead of going straight westwards to Pakistan. Others wondered about their fates and whether they would ever make it back to Pakistan. Nobody seemed to know where exactly we were in India or what day of the week it was. After a while, we became oblivious to everything except the constant rumbling and rhythmic gallop of the railway carriages.

Day in and day out, the train raced through the Indian countryside. We passed cities and villages. We crossed rivers and bridges. We passed houses, hedges, and ditches, but the old steam locomotive continued its arduous journey through the plains of northeastern India. At Kanpur Railway Station, some more POW carriages were added to our train, and from now on, the train's journey became even more laborious.

During this long and tiring journey, some people got sick. In the cold weather, a few of us developed the flu. Others got sick with dysentery. With only two restrooms in the cabin, sickness took its toll on all of us, and soon, the living conditions became unbearable. Sometimes, people vomited, and there was nothing to clean it up with. My friend Fayaz's grandmother, who was in her seventies, developed dysentery. She was old and frail, and after a day of severe diarrhea, she became dehydrated and died.

Fayaz's mother, Mrs. Khatoon, cried her heart out as Ammi tried to console her. No one knew what to do with the dead body, not even the Indian soldiers.

"Just dump her," I heard one guard say.

An older man among the refugees suggested, "We need to stop the train and bury her properly."

At the entire cabin's insistence, the guards agreed to the request. The train stopped in the middle of a deserted field.

Her body was wrapped in a white sari from Mrs. Khatoon's possessions. She was a smaller woman, so two guards picked up her body and started toward the exit.

"Where are they taking Nani?" Fayaz asked as he saw the men taking her grandmother.

Fayaz ran toward them crying, but a guard grabbed him before he could follow.

"I want to go with her!" He kept screaming at the men until they were out of earshot, "You can't just take my nani!"

Fayaz's father and several more guards followed with makeshift shovels. The grave was no more than a foot deep, just to keep the corpse from getting eaten up immediately by scavengers, though we all knew Fayaz's grandmother would end up that way. Fayaz's father offered prayers and read Fatiha as her body was laid in the shallow grave.

As we watched from the windows and Fayaz cried in his numb mother's arms, the men covered her body with a spattering of dirt. Without ceremony or headstone, she was buried, and the guards, apathetic to their job, returned to the train, and once again, we were off on our monotonous train ride to who knows where.

The train would stop intermittently to refuel, and then we would set off again. Mostly, the refueling would take place outside of the railway station out of fear of public retaliation against the POWs. The steam engine would halt under a water tower and would refuel for half an hour or so. Sometimes, when the train stopped in clear and desolate areas, we were allowed to get off the train under the watchful eyes of our guards and replenish our stock of drinking water.

We did encounter some angry mobs during our journey, but with us safely inside the train compartment, there was little they could do. At some stops, angry crowds of Indians would gather around our train and throw stones at us.

The wooden planks did indeed save us from shattered glass and injury. Sometimes, at night, we would hear the crashing sound of stones pelting the metal body of the carriage, and we would know that we were either passing through a station or a city railway crossing.

On occasion, the train would stop in the middle of a field or wilderness, and we would know that someone had died. Though we could not fully see outside due to the wooden planks, it became a routine that when someone died, we would stop in the fields, bury the dead body, and the train would move on.

We had completely lost track of the days. On the fifth day (the guard said it was the fifth day), we were told that there was room for us at a civilian POW camp in the Saharanpur district of Uttar Pradesh State of India. We were somewhat relieved at the prospect of an end to our miserable journey. The train chugged along towards Saharanpur in the foothills of the Himalayas.

For six days and six nights, the train continued its tedious journey. On the afternoon of the seventh day, we stopped at a farm. But after a while, the train did not move on, as was customary, and we knew we had arrived at our destination. This, we later learned, was a farm outside the city of Roorkee in the Saharanpur district of the Uttar Pradesh State of India. As of the year 2000, Roorkee is part of Uttarakhand State.

The train had stopped right in its tracks in the middle of a cornfield. In the distance, we could make out the silhouette of the Roorkee Railway Station. We descended the ladders at the front ends of each carriage and gathered in a small clearing. Each family stood in a small group with all their belongings in front of them. My family also lugged down our belongings and stood close to each other. Our brown leather suitcase, bistar bund, Rattan suitcase, small metal suitcase, and all five of us stood together.

We then picked up our belongings and started walking towards the green army transportation trucks lined up at the edge of the field. I climbed up the back of the military truck, and even with the tailgate down, it was quite a tall climb. We put our belongings on the truck bed and sat on our suitcases. The sun was setting behind the trees as the caravan of trucks started rolling. Soon rain started to pour, but, fortunately, the trucks were covered with a green tarp canopy. After a few minutes of a bumpy ride on an uneven dirt road, the convoy moved on to a paved road, and we picked up speed. We could see the lights of a small city in the distance, but otherwise, it was pitch dark outside due to the dense clouds. It didn't take long to reach our destination.

In the dark of the night, we disembarked and lugged our belongings into an army barrack. We were led to very large, dimly lit rectangular rooms. There was no furniture in the room, no fixtures or curtains, just barren walls and a long, empty cement floor. About ten to twelve families were put into each room. My head was spinning, and my feet were wobbly after almost a week of riding the train. It felt good to stand on firm ground after a long time.

We were wet and cold, and it felt very comfortable and safe inside the brick-walled barracks. We laid our belongings wherever we could find a space on the floor. We were exhausted after seven days of traveling on the train. We crashed on the floor, and sleep quickly overtook us.

12
POW Cage #1, Camp #34

The sun was up and shining fiercely when we woke up the next morning. We took our bearings and looked around. This, we learned, was Cage #1 of Camp #34 for the civilian prisoners of war in India. Our cage consisted of four old army barracks that had been vacated to make room for the refugees. The camp was located on the outskirts of Roorkee, which, in those days, was a small college town with nothing more than the College of Engineering and the Roorkee Cantonment.

Camp #34 was located inside the cantonment area. It consisted of four cages. Our cage was a large square-shaped area surrounded by an eight-foot-tall, barbed wire fence. The see-through fence was supported by metal pipe stakes ten feet apart, and the upper ends of the fence poles were covered with razor-sharp metal spikes. The top foot of the fence was angled inward at forty-five degrees to further deter anyone from climbing it. Whorls of barbed wire were laid around the bottom of each fence. Outside the barbed wire fence, armed Indian soldiers patrolled day and night with their big guard dogs. They carried World War II-era .303 Rifles with shiny blade bayonets mounted on the muzzles.

In each corner of the cage stood a tall wooden watchtower. Perched atop these towers, armed military guards watched us day and night and guarded against any attempt at escape. These soldiers carried machine guns and Sten guns. Large floodlights swept the grounds from the high guard towers to light up the nights. A horn loudspeaker mounted on a tall pole stood at each of the four corners of the cage to make occasional announcements.

Across the barbed wire fence of our enclosure were Cages #1, #2, and #3 of Camp #33. Camp #33 had only three cages, the last one being occupied by army and paramilitary prisoners. Our Camp #34 had four cages, so there were a total of seven POW cages in Roorkee. A dirt road ran between these camps and was patrolled by the Indian guards. Even more layers of barbed wire fences surrounded all the other cages so that the entire campus was heavily guarded and impenetrable. As it was, it seemed that our camps were quite isolated from the outside world, and there was not much population around.

Inside Cage #1, Camp #34 were four rectangular barracks, which were longitudinally oriented in a north-south direction. These were situated two together, side by side, at two ends of the cage, kitty-corner to each other. In the other two corners of the square-shaped cage were two large grassy fields, each the size of half a football field. The southwestern field was the smaller of the two and backed up to the officers' mess. With the exception of an old peepal tree in the northeastern field, there were few trees and little shade in our cage.

The barbed wire fence enclosed our cage tightly, and there was not much visible outside our fence, other than Camp #33 and the mighty peaks of the Himalayas to the north.

The only entrance and exit to our cage were at the southwestern corner, and this was flanked by two wooden guard posts. This gate was heavily barricaded with two more rows of spiked barbed wire fences, and it was guarded by armed soldiers twenty-four hours a day. To the right side of the entrance was the officers' mess, which was used as a common room for the more senior soldiers who guarded the gate. It was a small rectangular building with a gabled roof. The room was raised slightly above the ground, and a short flight of wooden stairs led up to the building. There was some basic furniture in the room, including a few chairs and desks.

To the left of the entrance was a large kitchen, or langar, where food was prepared for the residents of Camp #34. It was a rectangular brick building with dirty brown interior walls thoroughly covered with black soot. There were four giant firepits on a raised brick platform inside the kitchen, and one of these firepits was covered with huge, flat tawa for cooking volunteers to throw the giant flatbread roti. Fuel was placed through large holes on the sides of the raised platform. A large storage room stood next to the kitchen and held dry rations and fuel for the kitchen's fire pits.

A gravel road entered our cage at the gate at the southwestern end between the officers' mess and the kitchen and then turned north, dividing the cage into equal halves, each with two barracks. In the center of our cage was a single water tap surrounded by a ten-by-ten-foot shallow cemented enclosure.

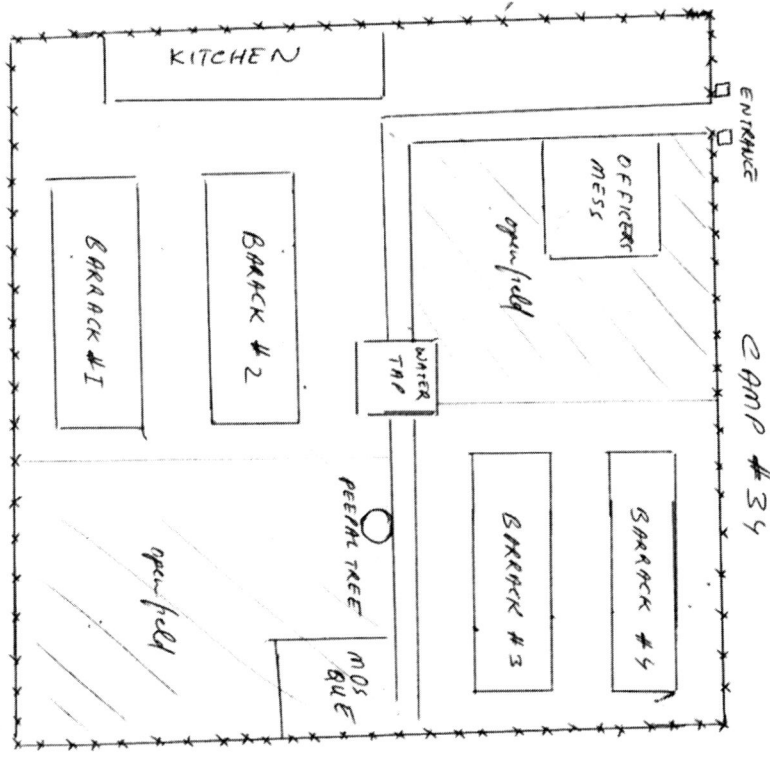

Figure 04: Map of Camp #34

The prisoners were housed in the barracks, which had been constructed more than a hundred years earlier to house the Bengal Sappers Regiment of the Indian Army Corps of Engineers. These were single-story, elongated, and rectangular buildings made of red brick. The inside walls were painted with white chalk paint, and a gabled roof made of long, corrugated sheets of asbestos, supported on wood trusses, provided cover. Each barrack was divided lengthwise into four rectangular halls, measuring about twenty by sixty feet each. These longitudinally oriented rectangular halls were connected by a small entryway or doorless passageway. Each of these four halls opened through two creaky, wooden hinged double doors into a covered common veranda that ran the length of the entire barrack. A row of wooden columns supported the asbestos roof on the veranda. Each wooden column was supported on a cylindrical cement base, and on the top, there were two wooden corbels to support the roof. This was the front side of the barrack. On the opposite side of our Barrack #1, small windows looked out at the backside of Barrack #2, which ran parallel to ours.

Figure 05: Sketch of the old military barracks that were constructed almost a hundred years ago.

On the south side of the barrack, there was a common bathroom for the men, and on the other end, there was one for the women. Each of the barrack's four halls housed about fifty or so refugees, which meant the entire barrack housed little more than two hundred people. The total population of Cage #1, Camp #34 was about 840. Little did we know, at that time, that this was to be our home for the next two years!

The first day was spent dividing each of the barrack's four rectangular halls between families, and we did so under the supervision of the Indian soldiers. There were a total of twelve families in our hall. Each family was given an area of about six feet by eight feet, barely enough for everyone to lie down side by side. We spread a stuffed blanket or a mat on the hard gray cement floor and covered it with a sheet. Then, we neatly arranged our suitcases and other meager belongings along the sides of our designated area to separate our space from that of our neighbors. It was like marking our territory. Pappa opened our bistar bund and laid it on our floor space, and then he put our suitcases around the perimeter of our area. We crisscrossed clotheslines across the hall so families could clip up bedsheets (like curtains) for privacy. It looked kind of cool, like a child's make-believe playhouse. This was my new home.

Once floor space was allocated along the four sidewalls of the rectangular hall to the families, a six-foot-wide passageway was cleared down the middle, leading in a wide U-shaped fashion from one veranda door to another. We would enter the hall through either of the two double doors, and the passageway provided easy access for us to just walk up to our designated floor space.

My new 'home' was six by eight feet of cement floor space in the southwestern corner of room four of Barrack #1. The two corner walls gave us some privacy, and there was a small glass-paned window in our section of the wall, which opened onto an alleyway that separated us from Barrack #2. This window had low clearance, so I could simply jump over the ledge to go out to play in the alleyway.

The 840 or so occupants of Cage #1, Camp #34 were all civilians. They were young, old, rich, poor, men, women, and children. Some were there with their families, while others were alone. They came from all walks of life. Some were well-educated, and others were illiterate. Some were merchants, managers, bankers, business executives, and some were peons, laborers, or truck drivers. Together, they made up what one refugee dubbed 'Mini-Pakistan'.

At the end of the first day, we were told to gather in the northwestern field to meet the Camp Commander. We wondered who that was and quickly gathered in the meeting area in the larger of the two grass fields. Soon, an army Jeep drove up the gravel road and stopped next to the water tap in the middle of our cage. Colonel Harnam Singh alighted from the Jeep and strode briskly toward the anxiously waiting crowd. At his heels was his assistant, Captain Ahluwalia.

13
Colonel Harnam Singh

Colonel Harnam Singh was a battle-hardened military man from the British India days. He wore the crisply ironed khaki green uniform of the Indian military, and an array of brightly colored war ribbons decorated his chest and shoulder straps. Underneath his tightly wrapped turban, a set of large, shining eyes, a heavy mustache, and a neatly netted beard adorned his gleaming round face. A short baton swagger stick with a small ornamental head and a 9mm pistol in a holster around his waist completed his elaborate attire.

Picture 18: Col. Harnam Singh when he immigrated to Canada after retirement.

A veteran of three Indian wars, Colonel Harnam Singh joined the British India Army before Partition and had seen action in Burma during World War II. He had retired two years earlier but was recalled to active duty at the onset of the 1971 war. Now that the war was over, his last assignment was to manage the POW camps at Roorkee before permanent retirement. A job that he was intent on completing with panache. This was to be the final plume in his cap, and he was determined to finish his long and unblemished career in the military in style.

The turbaned man spoke to the crowd in a loud and crisp voice. He certainly seemed like he was in charge, a man of clear authority. He greeted the camp residents and told us we would stay in the camp until arrangements were made to send us to Pakistan.

"I 'whant' to tell you…the Indian 'governa'ment' will take care of you. You are civilians, and we don't have anything 'againsut' you," he said at the top of his voice as he stood facing the crowd under the large peepal tree.

"Everyone in my camp will follow SOP." We did not quite understand what SOP was but later found out that it meant Standard Operating Procedure in military terminology.

"You will be treated well, according to the rules of 'Gineeva' con-ven-shun." He paused for a moment. "I will give you room and food, and you will be safe under my 'jurisdic-shun'. In return, I 'whant' good 'co'poration' from you." He told us that since diplomatic relations between India and Pakistan were severed, it might take some time for our transfer to be completed. We realized immediately that we were not just refugees; we were prisoners of war, too.

Harnam Singh promised that the refugees would be treated fairly. We would be fed, clothed, and provided with the necessities of life. But he made it clear, in no uncertain terms – that unruly behavior would not be tolerated and that law and order must be maintained.

"I 'whant' to tell you if anyone of you make trouble, then my name is Harnam Singh, and nobody mess with Harnam Singh!" His hands clenched on his holster, and the smile disappeared from his face.

He said everyone had to abide by the rules he would set. Those who did not follow orders would be punished with either solitary confinement or sent to 'fatigue' or forced labor. And if anyone tried to escape from the camps, he or she would be immediately shot. It was clear that Harnam Singh meant business. But at the same time, he made it known that good behavior would be rewarded and that he looked forward to establishing a good rapport with the civilian prisoners.

Over the next few days, brisk organizational activity ensued in a military-like fashion in Camp #34. Harnam Singh and his officers appointed room commanders from among the civilian residents. Then, from the four room commanders, a barrack commander was selected. On top of the barrack commanders, they also appointed a cage commander for the smooth and efficient functioning of our micro-community. The cage commander was responsible for everything that took place in Cage #1 and reported directly to Harnam Singh.

My father was one of the more educated people in the camp and had also worked in a managerial capacity at the Adamjee Jute Mills. So, my father was appointed as barrack commander. He was to report directly to Colonel Harnam Singh on all matters pertaining to the refugees in Barrack #1. We, as the children of the barrack commander, enjoyed a little bit of attention, though that was mostly of our own making as we felt rather important.

Our cage commander was a young and shrewd businessman from Dacca, Mr. Abdul Quddus Nagi. He was tall, fair, handsome, and tied his long black hair in a ponytail behind his back. In his early thirties, he was a well-articulated man who had a knack for communicating and getting along with people. Perhaps that is why Harnam Singh chose him to be the leader from among the prisoners. He was in charge of everything that happened in the camp, like the organization and assignment of duties among the prisoners, distribution of food, resolving disputes between prisoners, and forwarding their grievances to the Indians. Before the war, his family owned a mechanical engineering firm in Dacca that sold hydraulic pumps, tires, and auto parts. A bachelor himself, Quddus was in the camp with his sister and brother-in-law, who lived in Barrack #2.

With Mr. Quddus's help, refugees were organized into groups to perform various tasks in the camp. One group was assigned the task of cooking breakfast. Another was put in charge of lunch, and yet another prepared dinner. A group was enlisted to deliver food from the langar to the barrack rooms. Yet another group was responsible for carrying food supplies on their backs from the Central Ration Depot to the kitchen storage room.

Groups were also organized to clean the barrack rooms and toilets. For instance, a group was tasked with cleaning the windows and doors, and, as per Harnam Singh's instructions, every nook and cranny and corner had to be devoid of dust. A group of men mopped the long veranda and passageways inside each hall every morning. Then, there was a group that painted the veranda walls and outside walkways with white chalk paint once every few weeks. A group of men was tasked with cutting the grass in the two large fields, as well as picking up the trash in these fields. There was another group that brushed the pathways and cleaned the road that led into our cage. There was even a group to supervise all the other groups.

In short, every man in Camp #34 had a job to do every day – something to keep them occupied so they wouldn't have time for any other ideas. The women, however, did not have much to do. I guess Harnam Singh knew that men were more likely to cause trouble, and so he wanted to keep them busy.

Harnam Singh meant business. He was an organized, precise, goal-oriented military man, and he was determined to run Camp #34 with clockwork efficiency.

14
Settling into Our New Life

The captives of Cage #1, Camp #34 in Roorkee soon became accustomed to their new home. Surrounded by barbed wire fences and guarded by soldiers around the clock, we started living our new lives. Days and nights passed, and soon weeks and months slipped away. Thankfully, everyone was kept occupied by the numerous chores that Harnam Singh had organized for us, and we started to settle into our daily routine.

In the initial days of captivity, food was prepared in the langar by Indian military cooks. As time passed, Colonel Harnam Singh and his men selected volunteers from the refugees to do this job. These volunteers worked in three shifts to prepare food for the 840 or so residents of Cage #1, Camp #34. Food was cooked in huge 'deghs' placed atop massive fire pits and then distributed to the barracks three times a day.

We quickly adapted to our new lifestyle. Camp #34 became our new home. Sleeping on the floor in a room full of strangers no longer seemed strange. The presence of armed soldiers carrying guns with open bayonets patrolling just outside our cage became routine. And after a while, the spotlights sweeping down from the high watch towers late at night didn't bother us anymore.

I got used to my new 'home'. It was merely a six-by-eight-foot space with a floor mat and surrounded by our meager possessions. We sat, ate, and slept there. This is where I would always find Ammi. If anyone ever asked me where I lived, I would say, "Room number 4, barrack number 1!"

This was my home address.

We also became familiar with our roommates and the other refugees in the barracks. There were all sorts of people in Cage #1, Camp #34. There were old folks, and there were young. There was a very old couple in my barrack who talked little and kept to themselves. The old man walked hunched over, and with every step, his bones seemed to creak and moan painfully. No one knew what agonizing stories they hid under the deep wrinkles of their faces.

There were children of all ages in the camp. There were teenagers, toddlers, and infants, as well as young children of my age.

There were some single men in our camp, too; they were either bachelors or married men whose families were in West Pakistan. These men tended to band together in a group. There were some large extended families in the camp as well. One such large family spanning three generations lived in the last hall of my barrack. A large family of fair-colored ladies lived in my barrack, and my friends nicknamed them 'Dalda family' out of mischief because they looked as white as the Dalda brand of ghee butter. The families from Mr. Huq's house were still with us and were even in the same barrack as my family, but they lived in a different room.

Within a few weeks, the prisoners built a mosque at the far edge of the north field, close to Barrack #3. Adults and children all took part in the construction of the mosque. First, we selected a thirty-by-thirty square foot area facing Mecca. Then, we removed the grass and poured clay to create a firm earthen floor. A foot-high wall of mud, clay, and hay was raised on all four sides to enclose the prayer area. A small path was cleared from the gravel road to the masjid. A tarp cover was stretched on four poles to provide shelter from the sun to, at least, the front row. The prisoners petitioned the Indian Army camp administrators to procure a woven straw prayer mat for the floor. Most of the men offered prayers five times a day in the mosque, and on every Friday, a large congregation assembled for the Jumu'ah prayers.

Chacha was always seen in the mosque or, at least, close by. His family was in West Pakistan, so he didn't have much else to do other than hang around the mosque. He was an elderly Pathan from Peshawar, and he would always wear a white shalwar kameez. He had a long white beard and wore a white skullcap. Among his meager possessions was a large, round wall clock with Roman numerals. It looked quite out of place in our barrack hall, but once the mosque was built, the clock found its rightful place on the mosque's front wall. Chacha leaned it against the foot-high mud wall, and people would use it to check the time for the five daily prayers. Every morning after Fajr, he would wind the clock with a key, wipe the round glass face, and prop it back against the wall.

Between the mosque and the water tap, there was a large peepal tree. It was very old, and its wide-reaching branches provided much-needed shade from the sun. Nothing much grew under the tree, so men would sit down on the dirt around the tree trunk and socialize. The tree had large heart-shaped leaves and a large trunk that looked like many bundles of rope strapped together.

Under the large peepal tree was a makeshift barbershop. Bashir Hajjam had been a professional barber in East Pakistan, and his skills came in handy for the residents of Camp #34. He was quite a character and used to joke around a lot while trimming hair. I don't remember if his services were free for the refugees or if we had to pay to get a haircut.

Within our micro-community, there was also a cobbler. He, too, sat under the big peepal tree and worked a couple of hours every day repairing our broken footwear. His services were free and earned him the respect of both the prisoners and Col. Harnam Singh. Very few of us in the camp had proper shoes. In fact, most of us wore worn-out chappals or sandals, and it's hard to imagine how we could have survived without the shoe repair shop. Without his kind services, we would have been walking barefoot.

Every morning, I would wake up early and go to the mosque to offer prayers. I would then quickly wash my face using the Lifebuoy soap bar and brush my teeth. In those days, most people used charcoal powder to clean their teeth. We would procure charcoal waste from the langar and grind it into fine powder so it could be rubbed against the teeth with the index finger. It was an efficient and cheap way to clean the teeth.

We then waited for the food volunteers to bring in breakfast. While we waited, most adults would get ready for the upcoming day. Women would clean up their small floor space and tidy up the bedsheets. Men could be seen washing up or sitting in the veranda, shaving. I remember my father would also sit on the veranda floor and place his shaving bowl, brush, and soap on the floor. Then, he would prop a mirror in front and work up quite a lather on his face using his shaving brush and soap. It seemed to go on and on forever. It was quite a ritual, and I was fascinated to watch the swirling round and round motion of the brush gathering up a thick white lather.

After breakfast, we cleaned our home space again, and Ammi washed the couple of plates we had used. Then, she would offer Ishraq prayers and recite the Quran. It became quite a routine.

We also quickly became familiar with the daily roll call. Every morning, rain or shine, all men and boys over fourteen would line up in the open field on the north side of the cage close to the peepal tree. Here, the guards would count them to ensure no one had escaped during the night. I thought this was just a formality, but Pappa said it was one of Harnam Singh's tricks to kill time and keep us occupied. Some folks thought it was just another method of harassing us. Nevertheless, it was a clever way to gather everyone, make announcements, and keep everyone on the same page. After all, for Harnam Singh, it was all about following the SOP.

Picture 19: The turbaned Harnam Singh conducting his daily morning briefings under the peepal tree. In this picture, he is sitting on the right side as the prisoners sit on the ground and listen.

On occasion, someone would be missing from the morning fall-ins, and this would trigger a flurry of activity until the person was found. Invariably, someone had overslept or else was too sick to make it to the roll call. Young, old, or infirm, everyone had to wait in the field and would not be dismissed until each prisoner was accounted for.

Most of these early morning fall-ins were conducted by Captain J. P. Ahluwalia of the 5th Gorkha Regiment. Captain Ahluwalia hailed from Gurdaspur in Punjab. He was an intelligent, young, commissioned officer, probably in his thirties. He was always smartly dressed in his crisp khaki green uniform and a green peaked cap. Ammi said he must be from a good family since he respected the women. He would stand under the peepal tree with a few soldiers on either side for the morning drill while the prisoners lined up in the field facing him.

Another junior officer who assisted Ahluwalia was Captain Ajay Jarreth of the Signal Corps. He was a small-build, thin young man from Ferozepur and wore a light brown beret and a brown uniform. Captains Ahluwalia and Jarreth worked under Colonel Harnam Singh, who was overall in charge of running all the POW camps in Roorkee.

After the roll call and just before noon, we would have the daily rounds. Either Captain Ahluwalia, Captain Jarreth, or Col. Harnam Singh would walk the cage and inspect the grounds. They were always accompanied by a small entourage of heavily armed soldiers in khaki green fatigues. They would stop at the officers' mess, the water tap, the masjid, or just outside the barracks, and they would talk to the prisoners. Usually, a group of people would gather around them to bring up their problems and issues. Sometimes, children would follow the entourage, either out of curiosity or boredom. Perhaps they did not have anything better to do. Harnam Singh and his men didn't seem to mind; sometimes, they would even make small talk with the children trailing them.

On some days, they would tour inside the barrack halls, too. An unarmed Indian sepoy named Shastri would usually come in to warn the occupants that their barrack would be inspected soon so we would quickly clean up and put everything in order. Some would even quickly brush the floor and clean the passages between the matted areas on the floor. During the inspection, Harnam Singh would stop at some of the 'houses' inside the barrack halls and talk with the prisoners.

Shastri was a gangly and awkward-looking sepoy. He was one of the few Indian soldiers to venture inside the camp. He wore a crumpled khaki green uniform and a light green cloth cap. Shastri was probably a low-ranking Lance Naik or Havildar. Some people said he wasn't even that high of a rank; perhaps he was just an orderly or batman. He didn't carry a pistol or .303 rifle, just a stick. He was obviously not someone important and probably wasn't too bright either. Shastri had a knack for getting into trouble with his superiors in the Indian Army and would be reprimanded every few months. Prisoners would make fun of him because we could gauge the amount of trouble he had been in from the addition or removal of chevrons on his uniform.

Some of the children made fun of his stutter. He pretended to be friendly and tried his best to talk to everyone in the camp. He always tried to get cozy with the prisoners, especially the women. Silly Shastri was constantly sticking his nose into everything, so much so that we thought he was an Indian spy trying to get sensitive information from the prisoners. However, compared to the fierce soldiers who patrolled just outside the cages, he looked and acted very docile.

Mostly, the Indian Army officers were friendly toward the prisoners. Sometimes the adults would wonder why the officers were so nice to us since we were the 'enemy'. On the other hand, the lower-ranking soldiers, who were mostly assigned guard duty outside our caged enclosures, were not so nice and treated us harshly.

On occasion, Col. Harnam Singh would hold public meetings to hear our problems. He would stand on the stairs of the officers' mess, hands on his hips, almost touching the pistol in his holster, and address the prisoners. Mostly, people would complain about the long lines at the water tap or the lack of cleanliness in the restrooms. They would also complain about the quality of the food or the abundance of concretions in the rice or daal. Many complaints were related to improper living conditions, but sometimes people complained about their disorderly neighbors or other prisoners. During one such meeting, my mother asked Harnam Singh to install ceiling fans in the rooms because, in the summer months, the red-brick barracks would get really hot under the asbestos roofs. Harnam Singh would listen patiently to these complaints and show empathy, but I don't think anything much improved.

Three months into our captivity, the Indian government announced that all civilian POWs would receive a stipend of five rupees per month. As a family of five, we received twenty-five rupees for our personal needs. The military POWs were given a higher stipend in accordance with the Geneva Convention. The money came in the form of tokens, one and five rupees printed on colored paper, that could be used to purchase items from the Military Canteen Store. The canteen store was located about a fifteen-minute walk from our camp but within the caged complex and served all seven POW cages in Roorkee. It was run by a Bania, who was probably a civilian contractor. He was a small-built man who wore a white dhoti and kurta along with a round red cap on his head.

Some of the prisoners had bought in their heirlooms and jewelry or whatever precious stuff they could have salvaged during their escape from East Pakistan. As time passed, it became a real danger that these items could be stolen, and many were not comfortable just hiding such precious items within their allotted area in the barrack room. These concerns were relayed to Mr. Quddus, our cage commander, who arranged for the Indians to take possession of these valuable items for safeguarding.

A desk was set up in the officer's mess where two volunteers sat and made entries into a large black leather-bound register. The name of the head of the family was written down along with the number, type, and size of individual pieces of jewelry. Mr. Quddus supervised the entries and signed off against each item. The owner as well as the barrack commanders countersigned, and the register was sealed.

Once settled, the prisoners were allowed to write mail and to communicate with their relatives in the outside world for the first time. The Red Cross provided each family with an Indian airmail aerogramme envelope so they could write to their loved ones about their whereabouts. The printed aerogramme was an eight-by-eleven-inch paper that could be tri-folded to create its own envelope. It had a blue-and-red airmail border all the way around. The envelopes were stamped with prepaid postage and POW Mail in bold letters.

With tears in their eyes, the prisoners wrote their first letters, and some even prayed over the envelope to ensure its safe delivery. My family used our envelope to write to Ammi's parents in Hyderabad Deccan. The letters were then deposited in the officers' mess and taken away for mailing. One could only imagine my grandparents' jubilation when they received our letters and learned for the first time after many months that we were alive and in safe custody. A few weeks later, the return mail started trickling back into Camp #34.

15
Living in Oblivion

The prisoners of Camp #34 lived in oblivion. This was, in part, because we did not have access to newspapers and there were only a few radio sets in the camp, but the main reason was that the news we did hear was so painful that we preferred not to listen to the radio at all. In those days, the news was mostly about the 'Liberation of Bangladesh'. For us, that was a sad calamity, one that had severed an arm of our beloved country and landed us in these forsaken camps. There was abundant talk of the Indian victory and Pakistan's humiliating defeat. Then, there was the over-exaggerated propaganda of the atrocities committed by the Biharis and the West Pakistan Armed Forces that were so dear to us.

But there was no news about us, the 93,000 prisoners of war in the Indian camps. We felt forgotten and abandoned. So, we deliberately avoided the news hour, shutting ourselves off from the world around us.

The world outside Camp # 34 continued to revolve, though. While we were languishing in the camp, a lot was happening in the outside world. With the fall of Dacca and the liberation of Bangladesh, the Bangladeshi government, in exile, returned to Dacca on 24 December 1971. Their new prime minister-to-be, Sheikh Mujibur Rahman, had been arrested by Pakistani commandos a few months earlier and secretly imprisoned in West Pakistan. Following the defeat of the Pakistan Army in East Pakistan, there were serious concerns that Mujibur Rahman might be prosecuted or even murdered in captivity, but the Pakistani government caved to international pressure and agreed to return Mujibur Rahman to Bangladesh. We thanked God for his safe release since we knew if he had come to harm in Pakistan, we the hostages would all be in even worse trouble.

A week after our train had left Khulna for India, a triumphant Sheikh Mujibur Rahman returned to a hero's welcome in Dacca. Almost the entire population took to the streets to welcome the Bangabondhu, Friend of Bengal. He was sworn in as the prime minister of Bangladesh on 12 January 1972. Soon afterward, he announced that the Pakistani military officers who had committed 'crimes against humanity' in Bangladesh would be tried as war criminals. The Bangladeshi government started to prepare its case for a heavily publicized trial.

But now, the Indian government faced a dilemma. They had taken these Pakistani soldiers as prisoners of war and were obligated to protect them under international law. Handing them over to the Bangladeshi government for criminal prosecution would have meant that India had failed to protect its POWs. It was a difficult situation. So, the Indian Army quickly started moving the Pakistani soldiers out of Bangladeshi soil and into India, and by February 1972, the process was complete.

In March 1972, the Bangladeshi government announced a formal plan to try some 1,100 Pakistani military prisoners, but after a few months, the list was cut down to 195. The International Crimes Tribunal Act was passed by the Bangladesh Parliament, and plans were drafted for a formal trial.

After their embarrassing and devastating defeat on both the Eastern and Western fronts, the Pakistani government took an unusual stance. Pakistan refused to recognize Bangladesh as a sovereign nation, and the new prime minister of Pakistan, Zulfiqar Ali Bhutto, embarked on a world tour to convince allies not to recognize Bangladesh either. However, most countries joined India in recognizing the newly formed state. Bhutan, the Soviet Union, and the countries of the Soviet bloc were the first to recognize an independent Bangladesh, and the United Nations soon followed. The United States of America recognized Bangladesh in April 1972.

As our imprisonment dragged on, both the Indian and Pakistani governments blamed each other for our prolonged incarceration. But in reality, both Indian and Pakistani politicians were using our prolonged imprisonment for their own political gains. In Pakistan, Zulfiqar Ali Bhutto's government was still on shaky grounds, and he wanted to stabilize his position before letting almost a hundred thousand military POWs back in the country. He was unsure how the returning soldiers might react, and he was afraid that the disgruntled soldiers might destabilize his already fragile government or even try to overthrow him. In fact, most of the army officers from East Pakistan blamed him for their predicament; by failing to hand over the government to Mujibur Rahman after the elections, he had caused this division of the country. Many were angry and wanted to settle the score. Bhutto was wary of these officers and so wanted to move slowly.

In India, Indira Gandhi wanted to play to the Hindu nationalists by demonstrating her prowess in capturing almost a hundred thousand Muslim troops. She was proud of her accomplishments; she had dealt a crushing defeat to an old enemy and captured a large number of enemy troops and civilians. We were her trophy to show off. She was gloating in her victory and wanted to further humiliate Pakistan by prolonging our misery.

But the Indians soon realized their predicament. After their victory in East Pakistan, they had inherited the responsibility of containing and protecting almost a hundred thousand POWs. This was not something they had planned for, and within a few months, the cost of housing, guarding, and feeding the large number of prisoners became a mounting burden. They wanted to return these prisoners to Pakistan, but due to the war, diplomatic relations between the two countries had been severed. So, there were no channels open for dialogue to return the prisoners. India was clearly the victorious side in the thirteen-day war on both the Western and Eastern fronts. Therefore, the Indian government wanted Pakistan to make the first move.

Both governments began posturing and avoided direct negotiations. Pakistan blamed India for the prolonged imprisonment of the POWs and tried to score a diplomatic victory over India on the international scene. The government of Pakistan even issued a postage stamp with an iconic picture of prisoners, young and old, languishing behind a barbed wire fence. 'Prisoners of War in India: Challenge to World Conscience' was boldly written on the stamp in a move to pressure India.

Picture 20: Pakistan issues a stamp.

Finally, in July 1972, the Prime Minister of Pakistan, Mr. Zulfiqar Ali Bhutto, traveled to India seeking to repair damages from the war and to bring the POWs back home. Mr. Zulfiqar Ali Bhutto and the prime minister of India, Mrs. Indira Gandhi, met at Shimla, not far from where we were interned, and signed the Shimla Agreement.

The Shimla Agreement stipulated that both countries would settle their differences by peaceful means through bilateral talks and work toward the establishment of durable peace in the subcontinent. They also agreed to normalize relations and to promote trade, travel, culture, and communications between the two countries. India also agreed to return the territory captured on the Western Front to Pakistan. Bangladesh, however, did not take part in the Shimla meeting since Pakistan had not yet recognized Bangladesh as a sovereign nation.

During the civil war in East Pakistan, the Biharis, or Urdu-speaking people, had sided with Pakistan, as they shared a similar language and culture. Some had even taken part in the genocide of the Bengalis. When Bangladesh was created, these Biharis faced revenge at the hands of angry Bengalis.

There were almost two million Biharis in Bangladesh, but the Indians had taken only 78,000 military and paramilitary personnel and around 15,000 civilians with them and placed them in POW camps across northern India. The rest were left in limbo in Bangladesh. As the Indian Army started withdrawing from Bangladesh in March of 1972, any hope of these Bihari's return to Pakistan was buried. They were not welcomed in Bangladesh and branded as traitors. Pakistan was reluctant to accept them, fearing the country would not be able to cope with the economic burden of resettling almost two million refugees. Furthermore, it was physically impossible to transport such a vast number of refugees across a thousand miles to Pakistan.

These unfortunate Biharis were driven out of their homes by the Mukti Bahini and forced to live as stateless persons in refugee camps in Bangladesh. These camps were spread all over Bangladesh, but they were mainly concentrated in Rangpur, Mymensingh, Syedpur, Khulna, Brahmanbaria, and Chittagong. Here, the displaced Biharis lived in squalor in overcrowded conditions. We thanked God that my family were among the few thousand lucky civilians who were rescued by the Indians and transported out of Bangladesh, along with the Pakistani Armed Forces.

Living in Cage #1, Camp #34, we were cut off from the rest of the world. Our only sources of information were a few transistor radios. In the initial days of our captivity, there was no possibility of buying replacement batteries, so the owners would use the radios sparingly, turning them on only during evening news hours. We would listen to BBC World Service and Voice of America. At that time, the BBC Urdu news service was the most authentic source of news from the subcontinent.

The BBC South-East Asia correspondent Mark Tully was a household name in those days. He had extensively covered the aftermath of the 1970 elections, as well as the atrocities committed by the Pakistani military in the months leading up to the war in East Pakistan. During the war, his dispatches were broadcast all over the world as he traveled throughout East Pakistan and reported extensively from villages and towns. However, Pappa resented listening to the BBC and Mark Tully.

"He is always portraying us and our army like we are criminals."

"Is it really possible that our army killed all these innocent people?" Ammi asked one day.

"Of course! They did." There was repugnance in Papa's voice. "But not to the extent that has been reported. This is all propaganda. The figures Mujibur Rahman is giving are preposterous; they are exaggerating it ten times."

"I could understand if they fired on looters, hooligans, or terrorists, but if they killed any innocent civilians, that is unacceptable." Ammi sounded angry for the first time. "Why did our army go that far?"

"They were trying to prevent the breakup of our country," Pappa said as he prepared to sleep in our corner of the barrack room. "Frankly, I also wanted our country to remain united, but when the entire Bengali nation wanted to go their own way, they should have been granted independence. Sadly, our army went to the extreme, trying to impose their will upon the Bengalis."

"They never talk about the good things we did in East Pakistan." Ammi was heartbroken and dismayed. "Our contribution to the education and economic development in East Pakistan."

"And who cares about my sacrifices? My whole life, I dedicated to Adamjee Jute Mills, and now all is lost. We helped build this land from nothing. All the infrastructure and industries we established in East Pakistan."

"They always focus on the terrible and depressing events. The media is always sensationalizing the events, and that has just spread even more hatred." Ammi's jaws clenched; she was stressed.

"I still cannot believe how fast the hatred has come in between the Bengalis and Biharis. Only last year, we were like brothers and sisters."

For the most part, the BBC and VOA had accurately reported the events in East Pakistan. Both sides committed atrocities, and these news outlets presented both sides of the story. In the years leading up to the war, the Pakistan Army definitely committed more acts of aggression. In the later part of 1971, Mukti Bahini also retaliated and killed thousands of Biharis, but not to the same extent. So, the news tended to focus more on the brutal crackdown that resulted in the deaths of hundreds of thousands of Bengalis. But, somehow, we had refused to believe that our own troops would commit such heinous crimes. We still admired our soldiers and were blinded by patriotism. In some ways, we believed the media was responsible for our current situation and for spreading the hatred that ultimately led to the breakdown of the country and our current predicament. But what we didn't want to accept was that these news agencies were simply reporting the facts on the ground, and the fact was that the Pakistan Army had committed genocide. The reality was that the Bengalis had had enough, and they wanted to get rid of us, the Biharis and the West Pakistanis.

During the later days of the war, however, the BBC had made a huge blunder, which adversely affected the West Pakistanis and cemented our grudge against the media. Toward the end of the war, the BBC had erroneously reported that the Indians had airdropped five thousand paratroopers at Tangail near Dacca, when, in fact, they only dropped five hundred paratroopers. Reports of this 'massive' airdrop caused widespread panic among the top Pakistani military commanders and may have played a role in the quick surrender. We could never forgive the BBC for contributing to the surrender of our army.

Now, in the camp, we no longer trusted the news anymore. We felt we were the victims of the war and that we were being blamed for the terrible loss of lives in East Pakistan. Some of us did not want to listen to the news and chose to live in oblivion, cut off from the rest of the world.

16
Prisoner of War Camps in India

The 93,000 POWs taken in the aftermath of the 1971 Indo-Pakistan war were interned in camps all over Northern India. These were makeshift camps hurriedly commissioned to accommodate the massive influx of prisoners. There were about one hundred POW camps in India during that time, and each camp could hold between seven hundred and one thousand captives. The camps were located in the towns of Meerut, Jhansi, Ranchi, Agra, Allahabad, Sagar, Dhanna, Roorkee, Gwalior, Gaya, Ramgarh, Jabalpur, Fatehgarh, Varanasi, and Bareilly, among others.

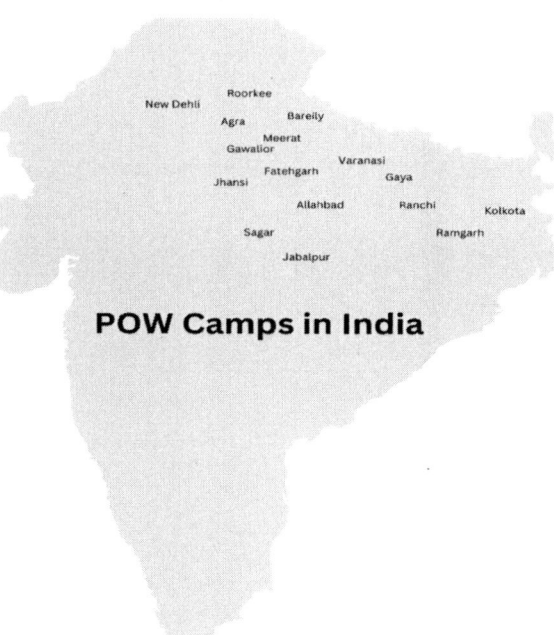

Figure 06: POW camps in India 1972–74

Housing such a large number of POWs brought into India from Bangladesh was no easy task. It certainly proved to be a challenge for the Indian government. This was the largest number of POWs taken since WWII, and housing and guarding all these prisoners required a Herculean effort. Makeshift residential facilities were commissioned across Northern India to house these prisoners. The prisoners were held in Indian Army cantonment areas or in prisons, or in some cases, in hostels outside of city limits. Mostly, they were placed in army barracks in old, barely used British-era cantonments. The perimeters were secured with barbed wire, and barracks were evacuated and refurbished to accommodate the prisoners. The areas around these camps were cordoned off and surrounded by many more layers of barbed wire fences. Watchtowers were erected around these camps, and extensive security measures were put in place to guard and contain the prisoners. In some cases, jails were remodeled to hold POWs, and some prisoners were housed in jails commissioned within some famous old forts such as the Agra Fort, Gwalior Fort, Fort William, and the Red Fort in New Delhi.

Most of these camps had only basic amenities, and the accommodations did not provide much more than a roof and walls for the prisoners. Most accommodations were old, dilapidated British-era army barracks that had fallen into neglect over a period of time. In many cases, the barracks lacked even functioning doors and windows. In Camp # 34, we were lucky to have proper toilets, but open trench latrines were the only option in some camps. While our camp had flowing tap water, others only had wells, and the prisoners had to pull water using hand pumps. Still, others just had an open water tank with a row of taps on two sides. Needless to say, living arrangements were very basic and rudimentary.

However, there was a 'Model Camp' in Meerut in Uttar Pradesh. This was an international relations gimmick put together by the Indian government, and the news media, foreign dignitaries, as well as delegations from the Red Cross and United Nations, were given a tour of this camp. Prisoners in this camp were given cleaner accommodations, better clothing, and were provided healthier food. They also had access to current newspapers, books, and other reading materials.

There was even a camp for the 'most dangerous' POWs. This was a high-security prison with multiple layers of extra safeguards.

The top brass of the Eastern Front of the Pakistani military were held in Fort William in Calcutta, Jabalpur Cantonment in Madhya Pradesh, Gwalior Fort in Gwalior, and the Red Fort in New Delhi. Later, most of them were moved to the Red Fort in New Delhi. Some of the more notable military POWs were Lt. General Amir Abdullah Khan Niazi, commander in chief of the Eastern Command, R. Admiral Mohammad Sharif of the Pakistan Navy, Air Commodore Inamul Haque, Major General Rao Farman Ali Khan, Major General Mohammad Jamshed, Navy Captain Ahmad Zamir, Lt. Commodore Mansur-ul-Haq, Commodore Tarek Kamal Khan, and Major Siddique Salik.

Of the 93,000 prisoners of war, the vast majority were military personnel. Almost 54,000 were from the army, about a thousand each from the Navy and Air Force, and 22,000 were paramilitary, reserves, or police forces. The rest were civilians. My family was among the 15,000 civilian refugees who had been picked up by the Indian Army during the evacuation of East Pakistan.

Army personnel and civilians were kept in separate camps. Military officers were provided with slightly better accommodation than the civilians. Some military officers had families with them in East Pakistan. The families were separated from the officers and kept in separate yet adjoining camps along with other civilians. They were allowed a thirty-minute visit from their wife or children once a month.

The military POWs occasionally received visits from local social, political, or religious figures, and sometimes journalists interviewed them. There are reports that some of these visitors were Indian intelligence operatives attempting to interrogate, brainwash, or recruit army officers for counterintelligence purposes.

In some camps, entertainment was also arranged for the more senior personnel, and there were occasional instances when sightseeing trips or musical programs were arranged for the military officers. In a camp in Meerut, the Hindu commanding officer presented the Quran to the POWs, and out of respect for the Holy Book, he had his Muslim sepoy distribute it among the inmates.

At the same time, there were reports of torture and mistreatment of POWs in the camps. The International Committee of the Red Cross reported cases of cigarette burns and nail pulling. Very commonly, the prisoners would be made to stand under the midday sun for hours, and sometimes they would be deprived of water or food for a few days or put on half rations for a period of time.

Other forms of punishment included forced physical labor, confinement in dark rooms, solitary confinement, and the intentional withholding of cigarettes, soap, shaving razors, or other personal care items. Often radio transistors were confiscated to punish us. Sometimes, the Indians would forcibly deprive the prisoners of bedding, floor mats, clothing, and personal items such as books and radios. In some instances, soldiers were confined to their barracks from sunset to sunrise and were not permitted to go out to the latrines at night. So, they had to evacuate themselves in buckets placed inside the barracks.

The commissioned army officers interned in the POW camps were assigned a batman or a jawan of the Pakistan Army to care for their needs. Unlike us civilians, the officers had access to newspapers and magazines, and in some camps, they could even request books or other reading material. The military men also received a higher stipend than civilians. Majors, colonels, and higher-ranking officers received a salary of 110 Indian rupees, while captains and lieutenants received 90 rupees per month. In contrast, the civilian prisoners were paid only five rupees a month.

Despite the extensive security measures taken to confine the prisoners, there were numerous escape attempts during the two-year period. Many young and spirited officers of the Pakistan Army felt it was their duty to attempt escape. They also knew it was the duty of their captors to prevent any such attempt and that they might be shot on the spot, but that did not deter them. Most escape attempts were made by digging tunnels under the living quarters with spoons, forks, or knives. The earth removed from the tunnels was quietly dispersed around the surrounding grounds. One could only imagine how difficult this must have been.

Most of the escape attempts were made from the camps in Meerut, Ranchi, and Sagar. A few were even successful. However, many escapees were soon caught and severely punished. And in almost all instances, the entire camp was subjected to a collective punishment. Not only was this meant to deter aspiring escapees but also to punish anyone who might have been aware of such escape plans and, thus, considered co-conspirators. These escape attempts also led to retribution in the form of tightened security measures, increased searches, and frequent roll calls, even in the middle of the night.

There were other instances of collective punishment of the whole camp for the foolishness of a few. Attacks on guards, acts of civil disobedience, and hunger strikes were also met with harsh punishments. As the imprisonment dragged on, more and more prisoners became restive, and tensions started rising between the POWs and their Indian captors.

Providing food for the 93,000 POWs was a mammoth task. In most camps, the jawans or civilian volunteers cooked food for the prisoners. But providing rations for the kitchen was an enormous task in itself. Large quantities of flour, rice, grains, and vegetables were brought in for the prisoners. Almost every day, milk and eggs were brought in for the children. Coal and chopped wood were delivered by the truckload.

In later days, meat was also provided to prisoners. Since the prisoners were all Muslims, they only ate Halal meat prepared in accordance with Islamic law. This meant that the Indian government had to make special arrangements to provide Halal meat to the inmates. Many camps were located on the outskirts of small cities, and Halal meat was not readily available in large quantities, so it had to be specially commissioned.

Senior officers of the Indian Army and government officials would sometimes visit the POW camps for inspection. Though the prisoners mostly lived in isolation, local dignitaries were sometimes allowed to meet with them. Later on, the Indians even allowed relatives to visit the prisoners in captivity under close supervision. Many prisoners were Biharis, who had migrated to East Pakistan from various parts of India and so still had relatives in India who could come to see them. In some cases, local Indians living in communities close to POW camps sent gifts to the prisoners on special occasions, like Independence Day or Eid.

The cost of housing, guarding, and feeding almost a hundred thousand prisoners was enormous. The Indians, already suffering from the economic cost of a war on two fronts, soon began to feel the economic burden of caring for the refugees, too.

17
A Kid's Wonderful World

Fortunately, there were a good number of kids my age in the cage, and we all kept one another company. My friends and I wandered around all day long and played cricket or football. We sat under the veranda and played our little make-believe games. Sometimes, we ran around for no good reason or played hide and seek. But we knew not to venture too close to the barbed wire fence. The fence was a constant reminder of our captivity, and we knew touching it or even going near it could land us in deep trouble.

In the initial days, we would make improvised bats and balls. For instance, we made a cricket bat by attaching a handle to a wooden plank with rope. My mother cut up old, ragged clothes and stuffed them tightly into a small round cover she had stitched until the ball was hard and round. That was my cricket ball. A larger stuffed ball worked just as well for soccer. Even with this improvised equipment, we enjoyed our games thoroughly.

We also invented a board game and played using caps from empty cream and toothpaste tubes. We would line up the caps with the smaller ones in front and larger ones in back, much like chess pieces. Then, we would advance these 'soldiers' across a smooth surface by flicking them with a finger. If our cap toppled the opponent's 'soldiers', that would be a victory. The game would continue until all of a player's pieces fell.

We played with miniature plastic animals, too. In those days, each box of Binaca toothpaste that our families purchased from the Military Canteen store came with a little plastic toy animal. It was probably just a publicity gimmick by the toothpaste company. Inside every carton, we would find a colorful replica of a lion, elephant, cow, dog, squirrel, or deer, etc. My heart would jump with anticipation and excitement whenever we opened a toothpaste box. I would collect these animals and proudly display the collection to my friends.

Some of us would brag about our extensive collections. We even traded the toy animals with each other and had a fun time.

We made slingshots from forked tree branches and catapulted small pebbles. That was a fun game. We used to shoot at birds and squirrels. Once, though, a young boy took aim at an Indian Army guard, and after that, they confiscated all our slingshots. I was sad that after this incident we were no longer allowed to play with slingshots.

Then there was Pittu. This game was played between two teams. The aim of the game was to use a ball to break apart a tower of seven flat stones stacked upon one another and then to remake the tower before getting hit by the same ball, now possessed by the opposing team. Instead of stones, we used fallen asbestos from the roofs of our barracks, which we chiseled into shape to make seven flat pieces. We not only lived under asbestos roofs for two years but also crushed and hammered them to chisel out flat stone-like pieces for our Pittu game. Back then, either nobody knew about the carcinogenic properties of asbestos or those who did know didn't care.

One of the coolest things we did was to go to the doctor. That was our only chance to leave the confines of our cage, and we almost looked forward to getting a sore throat or a stomach bug! One of the prisoners, Mr. Shaukat, was responsible for taking the sick to the Medical Inspection (MI) room, and we tried our best to impress him that we were sick and needed medical attention.

Every day, the other kids and I would meet in the rutted, north-side field to play. While I preferred cricket, others liked soccer better, so we'd switch. I was too slow to be a good soccer player, but I didn't let that stop me, nor did it stop any other kid, even if injury was involved.

"I'm open!" I shouted to Fayaz, who was trying to outrun Ali, the fastest boy in our camp.

Fayaz saw me at the last moment; he was nimble and stopped quickly and pulled his left leg back to kick the ball, but Ali was faster. Their legs collided and Fayaz went diving, face down, into the dust.

"Oh, man, you okay?" Ali asked. The athletic boy had managed to catch his balance while Fayaz had his spectacular wipeout.

I ran over to make sure my friend was okay, but Ali had already lifted him off the ground and was helping him dust off.

"Fayaz!" I huffed up to them and took a second to catch my breath. "You all right?"

He nodded. "Just a little wipeout."

He put weight on his left leg and grimaced. We helped him limp to the sidelines while all the other kids gathered around. I helped him wash the blood off his ankle and placed a fresh peepal leaf on the scrape.

The next trip to the MI room was almost three days away, and we had no way of knowing what was going on with Fayaz's leg. Mr. Shaukat, who, by now, almost acted like a doctor, pronounced a sprain and told Fayaz to stay off it for a couple weeks.

"There is no need to go to MI room," he declared. "I will give him a cream, and all will be fine." He reached deep into his shoulder bag and produced a jar of bright white ointment, which he gave to Fayaz.

I visited Fayaz daily, helped apply the cream that Mr. Shaukat had provided, and wrapped his ankle. It was the first time I had experience giving any kind of medical care, and I was hooked.

During our games, we would sometimes lose the ball under the barbed wire fence that surrounded the cage. It would usually get caught between the bottom of the fence and the whorls of barbed wires surrounding the bottom of the fence. The soldiers on patrol between the cages wouldn't let us retrieve them. We knew that if we went close to the wires or touched the barbed wires, we would be severely punished. None of the kids in the camp dared to retrieve the balls, and our precious balls would be lost forever. After a while, quite a few balls collected under the barbed wire fence of our cage. I would look longingly at them but did not dare try to get them back.

I was double-jointed, contortionist, and quite a show-off. My friends would tie both my hands behind my back, and I could rotate them above my head and bring them around to the front without breaking the grip. Fayaz said if anyone could squeeze through the gaps between the barbed wire fence and escape our camp, it would be me.

There were a couple of stray dogs that would occasionally squeeze underneath the fence and come into our cage. They looked quite emaciated, just like some of the prisoners; perhaps there wasn't much to scavenge around. Just as we were scared of them, they too seemed afraid of us and would run away at the slightest approach.

We loved to play with the dragonflies and damselflies that were quite abundant around the camp in some seasons. Some of my more agile friends learned to catch the dragonflies, and they would tie a thread to their elongated bodies. The dragonfly would then take off on a random flight, and we would run behind it; it was a lot of fun.

On some early summer nights, we even saw fireflies under the peepal tree. We would run around trying to catch these beautiful glowing insects. It was kind of dangerous because we had been warned not to go near the peepal tree at night. Some superstitious older women in the camp used to say that evil spirits wander under its thick canopy, and if anyone sat under this peepal tree at night, they would go 'crazy'. Like their souls would be possessed by the ghost of the peepal tree. But Ammi said that was an old wives' tale. She said people can get disoriented under the big peepal tree because its abundant leaves produce large amounts of carbon dioxide at night and no oxygen.

After playing around all day, I would go back to my 'home' in Room #4, Barrack #1 and be rejuvenated. It was such a nice feeling to be with my mother and father, and as long as they were around, I had no fear.

One of the greatest joys for youngsters like me was that there was no school. We could play all day and night without needing to wake up in the morning for school. After a few months, though, the refugees did create some semblance of a school for older children. It was a very rudimentary arrangement. Some folks from the camp simply came together and volunteered their time to start classes for teenagers. I, however, did not have to go since I was too young.

My older brother did attend these classes, and he learned mathematics, physics, and chemistry from his teacher, Mr. Islam. Mr. Islam had been a chemical engineer at the Dalda Ghee Factory in Dacca, and though he had been a chemistry major, he had strong knowledge of physics and mathematics. He was around forty, square-faced, of average height, and had a pleasant demeanor. He volunteered to do these classes pro bono every day except Sundays. Khusro Bhaijan excelled in these classes, and due to the solid knowledge base he gained here, he continued to excel in his studies in later years, gaining numerous distinctions and educational awards. The classes were held in Barrack #4, which featured a twenty-by-twenty room the other barracks did not have.

In the afternoons, Mr. Khushnood held Quran reading classes in the same room. These were intended for younger children like me. Mr. Khushnood had been a mechanical engineer with the Water Board in Dacca, and he started teaching the Quran to children pro bono. He was also in his forties with fair skin and a broad, stocky build. He had a round face with a black mustache and long, well-oiled black hair, and he always wore a pleated black Kufi cap. A thick-framed glass that has been broken and mended many times rested on his large nose. His family was in West Pakistan, so he was alone in the camp. He had a deep voice and could recite the Quran beautifully. He would sit cross-legged on the floor, and we would gather in a circle around him. Mr. Khushnood had a small staff on which he would lean with his right hand and peer down at his class through half-closed eyes from behind the thick glasses. The students knew he was watching everything, and even the slightest disruption was met with a swift rap from his staff.

Under Mr. Khushnood's supervision, I became very good at reading the Quran. I completed my first recitation of the Quran within a few months and memorized some short surahs from the Holy Book. I also started learning the art of recitation and became quite good at Qirat. Many other children finished their Quran recitation during this time as well, and Mr. Khushnood proudly conducted these Khatam-e-Quran ceremonies in front of our families. In the later days, we were even able to buy some sweets from the Military Canteen store for these celebrations. We would look forward to these ceremonies in the hope of getting the sweet treats.

My sister, Maliha Apa, did not attend any of the classes; she was ten years old when we first came to Camp #34. She stayed by Ammi's side all day, and for the most part, the two of them stayed in our home in Barrack #1. She often played with a ragdoll Ammi had made her. As time passed, we had more worn-out clothes, and Ammi made more ragdolls with old scrap cloth. Later, our grandmother sent materials to teach my sister how to cross-stitch.

Maliha Apa had long hair, which she wore in two braids and short straight bangs across her forehead. Ammi spent an enormous amount of time caring for my sister's hair, massaging coconut oil into her scalp, combing, and braiding. Ammi believed the coconut oil would make my sister's hair grow longer and thicker.

Though I had no formal education for almost two years, my parents did their best to educate my siblings and me. I memorized math tables and did simple multiplication and addition/subtraction exercises with my mother. I started learning Urdu for the first time since in school in East Pakistan we'd only been taught Bengali and English. Ammi had been a teacher in Dacca, and she started teaching us the Urdu alphabet. Later, we got some beginner Urdu workbooks, and I started writing sentences in Urdu for the first time.

Ammi used to tell me, "You better be a doctor when you grow up, so work hard and pay attention when I am teaching you." I was not too happy about that since none of my friends had to study with their mothers.

I also learned many English words and practiced my handwriting. We were able to buy some lined handwriting practice books from the Military Canteen store, and I remember spending hours copying the beautiful calligraphy from my uncle Mr. Abid Hussain Qureshy's wedding card, which had come in the mail. He was living in England at that time, and my grandmother sent us the official invitation, perhaps only to share some happy news with us. In those days, we were desperately looking for any good news, and the announcement of his wedding brought us joy. I learned to write English beautifully in cursive by copying letters from the wedding card.

One morning, I was playing pittu in the dirt alleyway between barracks #1 and #2 when I heard a commotion. I ran with my friends to the field, and we saw a large number of military jeeps and cars parked next to the water tap. Col. Harnam Singh, Captain Ahluwalia, and Captain Jarreth were all there, and in the midst, there was an older gentleman who wore the crispiest uniform, and many medals and straps hung from his chest. He looked like someone very important. Later, we found out he was a brigadier in the Indian Army who had come to inspect our camp. He watched the morning roll call with Colonel Harnam Singh and talked to some of the prisoners. He seemed very pleased when he left, and the next day, he came again with his teenage daughter, who seemed very nice and talked to me and my friends.

Overall, life in the camp was not too rough for kids my age. I was carefree and contented, and for the most part, I played with my friends and didn't complain. After playing outside for long hours, I would come home to my barrack and crash on the floor. It was so comforting and even rejuvenating to bask in my mother's embrace. And even though I would occasionally have nightmares about Mukti Bahini coming to kill us, I was overall content and happy and just glad to be with my family.

18
Eat, Play, Pray, Sleep

Food was an important part of camp life, and many of our daily activities revolved around it. We ate the day's three meals, played in the fields, and prayed in the mosque. When night came, we slept. The three mealtimes and the five daily prayer times nicely compartmentalized our days and kept us occupied.

Food was prepared in the langar by volunteers and distributed to all the barrack rooms three times a day. Most of the kitchen volunteers had no previous cooking experience, so at first, the food was mediocre at best. But after months of practice, these volunteers learned by trial and error, and toward the end of our stay, the quality of food improved considerably.

The volunteers worked almost round the clock to prepare the three daily meals for the inhabitants of Cage #1, Camp #34. Food was cooked in massive fire pits in the langar. The fire pits were fueled by big logs of wood, and it would get very hot inside the langar. The volunteers had to work through smoke and flying cinders to prepare food. Curry and rice were cooked in giant pots or deghs that were so large that a person could almost sit inside one. The roti was made on a huge round tawa, and it was quite a sight to see the volunteers throw and toss the flattened dough on the convex surface of the tawa to cook large round rotis.

The kitchen volunteers not only cooked food but also procured and prepped the raw materials and arranged delivery of the cooked food to the individual barracks. Each morning, a group of volunteers carried into our camp the perishable raw materials for the kitchen from the Central Supplies Depot. These volunteers would leave at around 6 a.m. under a heavily armed escort and return a few hours later, carrying sacks of raw food materials on their bare backs. The dry rations were kept in a storeroom behind the kitchen, which was always full of onions, potatoes, grain, lentils, and flour. Chopped wood and coal were brought in every week by Indian Army trucks and piled up in an open storage area behind the kitchen.

Another group of volunteers was assigned the task of delivering food to the residents of the four barracks. These volunteers would bring food three times a day and distribute it to the residents in their 'homes' inside each of the halls. They would carry the roti in a big cane basket and the salan or daal in an aluminum bucket. They would bang the bucket with their serving spoons so everyone knew it was 'food time', and we would set out our plates in front of our makeshift 'homes'. My family had some enameled tin mugs and dark blue 'tamchini' plates that the Red Cross had given us in Dacca, and Ammi would put one out, too. Starting at one end of the room, they would use a big wooden ladle to dump food onto each family's plate. They would start at Room #1 and continue to the other end until the entire barrack got their meal. Each family would get a scoop of curry and roti, and we would all sit together on our floor mat and eat from the same plate. If a family was not in their 'home' to receive the delivery, they would go hungry. So, we made sure to be in the barrack room at mealtimes.

Picture 21: A family of prisoners eating together inside the barrack room.

I loved breakfast because it was always sweet; we would usually get orange marmalade along with puri. The volunteers would bring marmalade in large military-size tin cans and give a small scoop to every family. The orange peel marmalade along with hot, crisp, fried puris always tasted delicious. Chai or milk tea would be served with puri and marmalade. Every morning, the piping hot chai was brought in metal buckets and served with breakfast. Children would get milk at breakfast time, and I would put out my blue enameled tin cup in anticipation. Later on, Ammi asked the Military Canteen store Bania to stock Horlicks as well, and that made the milk taste even better.

For the other two meals, we were served either chapatti or rice along with curry. The curry would be either daal or potatoes or sabzi that had been quickly thrown together by people with little experience in doing this job. Most days, we were served one kind of daal along with chapatti. For daal, we would have split peas, masoor, black chana, arhar, urad, or moong. We became accustomed to so many different kinds of daal that we hadn't even known existed.

Potatoes were frequently served to the prisoners, too. We always ate potatoes with skin because no ration could be wasted. Russet potatoes were cooked in thin gravy, while sweet potatoes were boiled and served with rice. We had all kinds of curries, and for the most part, the curries were little more than watery gravy, and one had to search hard for lentils, vegetables, or small potato pieces at the bottom of the plate. Often, we would find little pieces of stone or gravel in the rice and lentils, so one had to chew carefully. On occasion, we found tree leaves or grass in cooked vegetable dishes. Ammi said the Indians were mixing a lot of grass shoots in the palak to make up for the bulk supplies that were needed.

The quantity of food handed out to each prisoner was nominal. Unlike the military POWs, who were given proper food according to the Geneva Convention, we received only the bare minimum sustenance food, which meant that each civilian prisoner got one chapatti and a small amount of curry at each meal. Some people in our cage lied and made all kinds of excuses to get a little more gravy from the distribution volunteers. I had a hard time swallowing the dry chapattis barely moistened with a very small amount of gravy. I was so fed up with the dry morsels that I made a promise to myself that if I ever got out of prison, I would eat lots and lots of curry and very little bread!

The man in charge of all the supplies to Camp #34 was Quartermaster Roshan Lal, a tall and dark-skinned non-commissioned officer from Punjab. From flour to onions and from fuel to blankets, he was in charge of providing everything to the prisoners. A thoroughly corrupt and unscrupulous man, he quickly figured out that he could steal flour and other non-perishable items from the camp and sell them in the black market in Roorkee. When the prisoners found out, they confronted him and threatened to inform Harnam Singh. Cornered, he pleaded for forgiveness. Finally, Mr. Quddus made a deal with him that in lieu of the stolen flour sacks, he would provide us with extra powder milk for the babies. The extra milk could not have been brought in through the regular India Army supply channel, so Roshan Lal made arrangements for the Bania to give extra powder milk to Mr. Quddus every month, who in turn distributed it among the mothers.

Toward the end of our captivity, meat was added to the menu. A stew was prepared in the langar that was to be the prisoners' first taste of meat in thirteen months. It was a big event, and the prisoners were visibly excited in anticipation. That evening, everyone waited eagerly in the barrack rooms with plates in hand, and when the distribution crew arrived, all eyes were glued to the food buckets. That day, the volunteers drummed the buckets even louder with their wooden ladles. As they started serving, the appetizing aroma of meat stew filled the air. Some prisoners even started imagining savoring the food.

The only problem was that, by the time the distribution crew reached the end of the room, they had run out of meat. The last few people got only watery stew. There was an uproar. Some furious men started shouting at the distribution volunteers. My friends, who lived at the back of our barrack, did not get to taste any meat after all that buildup of excitement. These little children silently ate their roti with plain gravy, tears of disappointment clearly visible in their eyes.

In Barrack #2, a different type of saga unraveled. By the time the distribution crew had completed their rounds and everyone was served, two pieces of meat were left at the bottom of the bucket. Nobody knew what to do with the two remaining pieces of meat. A fierce argument erupted, and all the prisoners started claiming their rights to the leftover meat. The last people to get served said they deserved the two pieces because it was destined to be theirs since everyone else was already served. An older gentleman said he should get it because he was the oldest, and another said he had the largest family. It almost came to a brawl, and someone ran to inform the cage commander.

Mr. Quddus came running into pandemonium. He looked down at the two lonely pieces of meat at the bottom of the bucket and then looked at the angry crowd gathered around him. He hesitated for a moment, and then the quick-thinking Quddus quickly grabbed the two pieces of meat with his hand and tossed them out of the door right into the jaws of the two stray dogs who were drawn in by the aroma of meat just outside the barrack door. Everyone's jaw dropped! Some people looked bewildered, and others chuckled under their breath. But at least the problem was solved.

The next week, however, we were prepared. Chacha had come up with a clever solution that seemed fair and equitable to everyone. When the food bucket arrived, he took command.

"Bring the balti over here." He pointed with his right hand to the center of the walkway inside our barrack hall. The food distribution volunteers looked perplexed.

"Put it down, put it down," he said as the volunteers slowly lowered the buckets on the floor.

By now, everyone in our room had gathered in the center to look at what was happening. Chacha placed two large empty bowls that he had brought next to the balti and asked everyone to move back.

"OK! Take the meat out of the bucket and place it in one bowl and put the potatoes in the other," he ordered.

As two volunteers sifted the meat and potatoes out of the bucket, he counted the pieces on his fingers. The process continued until only gravy was left in the bucket.

"Now that is good." He seemed satisfied as he looked at the bowls filled up to the brim with potatoes and meat.

"Now, each family bring your plates over here," he said. "I will give you the meat now." Chacha then distributed the meat and potatoes in equal proportion to the number of people in each family. Everyone was relieved to see this 'clever' solution and breathed a sigh of relief.

From that day on, tall tales of Chacha's wisdom circulated throughout the camp. He was clearly the wise old man, and people began going to him for advice and even to discuss personal problems.

From now on, every Wednesday was meat day, and as a result, Wednesdays became very special to us. For those dinners, we would get either chicken or mutton curry, hit items among the captives.

I remember one cold, wintery morning, piping hot chai was being served in our residence hall. As usual, the distribution volunteers worked their way down the length of the barrack, ladling tea into waiting cups. The residents quickly gulped down the tea, as it felt good in the chilly weather. However, this time, it tasted somewhat different. By the time they reached the end of the barrack and the level of tea dropped, the volunteers found a dead mouse at the bottom of the tea bucket. Pandemonium broke loose. Everyone started to puke. All along the veranda, I could see men and women, young and old, trying to make themselves vomit up the tea they had just consumed. It was quite a scene.

Some occupants of our cage became quite entrepreneurial. They started making snacks and nibbles such as samosas, choley, or jalebi and selling them to the other inmates. They either bartered the items or traded using the paper token money we got as our monthly stipend. In order to cook these items, they made small stoves in empty metal paint buckets. We had plenty of empty paint buckets lying around since one group of prisoners was constantly covering the walls in white chalk paint. The top of the paint bucket was propped up with three nails to hold the cooking pot, and an opening was cut along the side of the pail to allow for wood and fuel to be put inside. The inside wall of the bucket was then covered with clay to make an improvised stove. It served the purpose quite well.

My family made a stove, too, and on occasion, my mother would cook samosas and chaat. My brother, Khusro Bhaijan, learned to make potato rolls and other fried snacks by watching other people do it. Then he would invite his friends to a party. There was a yard behind the langar where semi-burnt coal and wood logs from the big kitchen fire pits were dumped after midnight in preparation for a new fire for the breakfast next morning. My brother would sneak over in the dark of night to pick this leftover fuel for our own stove. He would boast about his adventures in the middle of the night to me and my friends, telling us how dangerous it was to pick up embers still hot from the fire pit.

19
Life Goes On

The people in Cage #1, Camp #34 came from all walks of life and backgrounds. But as months passed, they became friends and developed a sort of camaraderie. They cared for one another and looked after each other's needs, and despite the fact that we'd been herded together into a room with no walls or boundaries, everyone tried their best to be respectful and to allow others their privacy. We became like a large family, and for the most part, people got along quite well. Small disputes were settled amicably. Since my father was the barrack commander, his advice was always heeded when resolving conflicts, and people respected him.

Soon, the prisoners became accustomed to their new lifestyle. Despite our internment, life went on. We celebrated the special days and the Holy Nights of the Muslim calendar by praying in the mosque. People prayed through the Holy Nights until dawn. The mosque was decorated with bunting and candles bought from the Military Canteen store for these special occasions. Incense sticks filled the air with a pleasant aroma. Sweets, too, were either prepared or bought from the Military Canteen store for these auspicious nights.

Both Bakra Eid and Eid ul Fitr were celebrated with great enthusiasm and fervor. People wore their best dresses and greeted each other cheerfully. Almost everyone in the camp would turn up for the Eid prayers, and the lines in the mosque would extend beyond the mud wall perimeter and into the nearby field. After Eid prayers, people would visit each other.

On some of these special occasions, Bara Khana, or The Big Meal, was served in the army tradition. The langar would prepare a special meal, which, in most instances, was still the same lentil or vegetable dish, just garnished with onions, oil, mint, or coriander to make it look 'special'. Bara Khana used to come with a side of a sweet dish, too. The sweet dish would invariably be sooji ka halwa, a simple dish made by cooking semolina powder in water and sugar. Occasionally, raisins and cardamom were added for flavor. In the later part of our captivity, meat was added to the Bara Khana menu, too.

Other big occasions in the camp were Bismillah (the ceremony marking the start of learning to recite the Muslim Holy Book) and Khatam-e-Quran (the ceremony marking the completion of recitation of the Muslim Holy Book). These ceremonies were held in Mr. Khushnood's Quran classroom. A few weddings even took place during our captivity. These were very low-key events with just the nikah, or affirmation of marriage, by both bride and groom and attended by only a few close family members. There was no formal celebration or food involved.

The prisoners kept themselves occupied. While the children played cricket, pittu, and hide and seek, the adults took their sports more seriously. Captain Jarreth had a net installed at one corner of the northern field and provided the prisoners with a volleyball. The adult men formed teams and arranged proper tournaments. Each barrack had a volleyball team and a soccer team, and they held regular games. Cricket was another popular game, and the adults chipped in to buy a cricket bat and ball from the Military Canteen store. It was a special-order item, and people eagerly waited for three weeks before the bat and ball finally arrived.

A group of men took up bodybuilding. They would gather every morning at daybreak and lift weights. These weights were made by pouring cement into empty paint buckets. They simply lifted the weights using the bucket handles. They also made barbells by sticking a bar between two cans filled with cement. Another group of men played kabaddi, a popular contact team sport in India, in which players would take turns chasing and trying to touch members of the opposing team without getting captured. The objective of the game is for a single offensive player to run into the opposing team's half of the court, touch out as many of their players as possible, and return to their own half of the court, all without being tackled. These, along with volleyball and cricket, were the most popular sports in our camp.

Some older folks took to walking, and in the evenings, they could be seen making laps around the northern field. Many married couples used to walk, too, and perhaps these were the only moments they could spend in private. Ammi and Pappa also used to walk almost every evening after dinner.

The more intellectual men took up chess. Others played card games like Bridge, Rummy, and Poker and held regular games and tournaments. My friends and I would gather around the players and watch these games intently.

Many male refugees were hooked on cigarettes. But as cigarettes were expensive, they purchased beedi from the canteen store. Beedi was the poor man's cigarette and was made by wrapping tobacco flakes in dried leaves. However, some of the refugees bought actual cigarette paper and loose-leaf tobacco from the canteen and rolled their own cigarettes. In the evenings, many young men would be seen enjoying a smoke along the verandas and in the grounds.

We became good at improvisation. Since eating and relishing the paan was a popular tradition in East Pakistan, many prisoners had been in the habit of chewing the paan, and they missed it terribly during our incarceration. Betel leaf was not available in the camps, so many people began using green leaves from the peepal tree instead. They would wrap chopped betel nut and slaked lime in the peepal leaf and then chew it as paan. This was a favorite pastime for many in the camp, especially the older women.

Healthcare provisions were meager at Camp #34. Anyone who got sick had to be taken to the Medical Inspection (MI) room located almost half a mile away in the center of all four camps at Roorkee. It was a long walk for the old and the sick, and those who could not make it on foot were often carried by relatives on a field stretcher. Mr. Shaukat Ali, a former dealer of Vespa Scooters in Dacca, was in charge of the MI room contingent from our cage. He was a short, stocky, middle-aged man, and he took his duties very seriously and with great pride. Somehow he had procured a red-and-white Red Cross armband, which he wore proudly all the time.

Every Monday and Thursday morning, Mr. Shaukat would gather the sick and infirm at the entrance of Cage #1. He would line them up in a single file in front of the barbed wire gates and walk up and down the column, inspecting them and counting them as if he were an army general inspecting his troops. Then they would proceed single file through the barbed wire gates and into the narrow, fenced corridors between the cages. Guarded by soldiers carrying .303 rifles with open bayonets, the sick and the infirm would make the slow and tedious journey to the MI room and back again. Mr. Shaukat would always be seen swaggering at the front of the line.

The MI room was located about half a mile away within the caged complex of the Roorkee camps. An Indian military doctor oversaw the MI room. He became good friends with Mr. Shaukat and provided him with some basic medications and creams, which he carried around in a small shoulder bag made of jute. So, Mr. Shaukat became quite an expert in treating minor ailments and emergencies such as colds, nausea, diarrhea, pain, or even minor injuries. Those who got really sick had to be admitted to the Military Hospital (MH) in Roorkee. The MH was located not too far from our camp and was within the cantonment area. A few very sick or very old people died during our stay, and they were buried in an old Muslim cemetery very close to the camps.

The other contingent to leave Cage #1, Camp #34, on a weekly schedule was the group that went to the Military Canteen Store or the Commissary Store. Here, POWs could buy supplies with the five rupee coupons provided by the Indian government. Each Wednesday morning at 10 a.m., a group of prisoners would line up in a single file at the main entrance and then set out on foot to the Military Canteen Store. Guarded by armed Indian sepoys at the front and rear of the convoy, they would make their way through the serpentine rows of barbed-wired fences between cages to the store, which was located about a fifteen-minute walk from our cage. The prisoners would buy essential food supplies since the food and milk provided by the Indians were insufficient. One could also buy many 'luxury' items here, including cigarettes, toothbrushes, toothpaste, soap, shaving cream, razor blades, and other personal care items. Other hot items were radio batteries, South Asian pickles, candlesticks, matches, and coconut oil.

The shopping expedition was quite a treat, and some prisoners found any excuse to go to the store each week. I, however, wasn't allowed to go, as only adults were permitted. I remember eagerly waiting for my father to come back from the store with my favorite cow milk toffees.

Apparently, the store was a tiny shack of tightly packed rows of wooden shelves. The shelves were haphazardly filled with glass bottles and boxes, whereas grains and spices poured out of the widely open mouths of jute bags scattered on the floor. Ammi said the Bania's shop had a distinct sweet pungent smell that was a mixture of cooking oil, chickpea flour, incense sticks, and soap bar.

The proprietor of the canteen store was a miserly young Bania. Nobody knew what his real name was, but since he belonged to the Bania Indian merchant caste, everyone called him Bania. He wore a white stitched cloth cap and a dirty white dhoti and kurta. He would sit cross-legged on a stool behind his desk, and a large, framed picture of Lakshmi (the Hindu Goddess of Money) rose behind him. He had put a garland of yellow plastic flowers around the picture frame and surrounded it with burning incense sticks.

The young Bania was abrupt and terse but an enterprising and conniving businessman. He would find every opportunity to swindle the prisoners and make a hefty profit from every item in the shop. On occasions, he would take special orders and procure items like halwa or traditional Indian sweets from outside and charge the prisoners an arm and a leg.

Though Bania was a crafty and cunning man, he became a blessing for the prisoners. He was greedy and would do anything for money.

"Give me enough money, and I will get bird's milk for you," he was known to have said.

So, the prisoners started giving him money, trinkets, and small jewelry items in lieu of food and other supplies. On one occasion, I am told, he even procured abortion materials for a young POW girl who got pregnant out of wedlock. Few of the prisoners had somehow gotten hold of some Indian currency (it was probably smuggled in through the Indian guards), and though Bania was only permitted to accept tokens, he would accept currency when no one was watching.

Once a week, an Indian military truck would take volunteers to the Roorkee Railway Station to get coal and wood for the kitchen. They would spend hours manually loading coal into the truck, and by the time they got back, their skin and clothes would be blackened with coal dust. It was hard, intense work. But the prisoners still fought each other to go to this fatigue, as it was a good excuse to leave the cage even for a few hours.

A lot happened around the lone water tap of Cage #1, Camp #34. The tap was located in the center of our cage and was a focal point for many activities. Around the water tap was a ten-by-ten-foot cemented drainage area surrounded by a raised concrete slab. Men would shower under the tap and wash their clothes. Sometimes, women also gathered there to wash clothes and gossip. Some ladies developed quite a reputation for gossip, and most people learned to stay away from them. We would bring our Surahis every morning to fill up with drinking water. In summer, there would be long lines at the tap.

Taking a shower under the water tap was quite a chore for the men. We would just cover our private parts with a loincloth and shower. There was always a long line and no privacy as we showered under the open sky. In winter, we had to shower in ice-cold water. It was hardly my favorite thing to do, and, in fact, most people only showered once every week or two.

The women's restroom was located at the northern end of the barrack, and, for the most part, they washed their clothes and showered there. The men's restroom was at the southern end of our barrack. The restroom facilities were very old, broken, and dirty. Since they were so small, we preferred to wash our clothes outside at the tap. Many women shied away from washing clothes in front of onlookers in the center of the camp, so it became a job for the men. We hand-washed our clothes using soap and water, rinsed them under the tap, and then wrung them tight to get the water out. Then, we would hang them to dry on a clothesline inside our barrack room. There was no iron in the camp, so we wore our clothes with wrinkles.

Most people in the camp took siestas. My mother ensured that I also took a nap in the afternoon, and I remember waking up to start my evenings fresh. Perhaps we did this out of boredom, but it was certainly a good way to pass time during the long summer days.

On dull and doleful days, small groups of prisoners would be seen roaming aimlessly around the cage. Sometimes, they would sit and chat, probably talking about the old days and their lives in what was once East Pakistan. Almost everyone had fond memories of the homeland we had just lost. However, the groups had to be small because if the guards saw more than six people together, they would shout across the cage fence to break up the assembly.

Life goes on in captivity. Love and romance bloomed, even in barren Camp #34. Some teenagers got the love bug, and, of course, there were romantic escapades. One such Romeo was a young man named Saleem. He was nicknamed Prince Salim, in reference to the Mughal prince who was famous for his romantic affairs with Anarkali. He had a brass harmonica that he often played at night. My friends used to say that when he puts the harmonica on his lips, the melodious tunes coming from this little mouth organ would magically win over the heart of any young maiden.

During our internment period, many couples got engaged and even married. These would be simple ceremonies conducted by Mr. Khushnood.

The newlyweds were given some privacy for their honeymoon. Mr. Khushnood's Quran studies classroom served as the 'honeymoon lodge' for these newlyweds after school hours. We even welcomed six or seven babies during our imprisonment. One of these babies, a little girl, was named 'Roorkee Begum'.

Pregnant mothers were given little better food than the rest of us. They would get additional milk and boiled eggs, and some of my friends joked that women were getting pregnant in order to get better food.

There was an incident when a young man indecently touched a teenage girl. Some people saw it happen, and immediately there was an uproar. Tempers raged, and the aggrieved girl's family was ready to fight for their honor. The news quickly reached Col. Harnam Singh, who got alarmed at this incident. He decided to mete out an exemplary punishment to prevent similar incidents. The young man's head was shaved, and his face and body were covered in black soot from the kitchen. He was, then, handcuffed and paraded by an Indian Army sepoy through each room of the four barracks. Needless to say, as a result of the stern punishment, this kind of behavior was not repeated during the rest of our stay in the camp.

The civilian leaders of our cage, including Mr. Quddus, Mr. Dawood, Mr. Nasim Buti, Mr. Abdul Hai Piracha, and my father, made quite an effort to maintain a good relationship between the civilian prisoners and their Indian captors. Mr. Quddus was very tactful and obtained many concessions from Harnam Singh that were perhaps not available in other POW camps. To maintain an amicable relationship and please the Indian officers, they even threw a party during the Indian festival of Raksha Bandhan.

A sumptuous dinner was prepared in the langar. Fish was procured for the first time ever in our cage through the courtesy of Bania. Daal and rice were made with a lot of spices, and dahi vada (fried flour balls in a yogurt sauce) was prepared for the occasion. Dinner was served in the officers' mess, and the Indian officers brought in their wives along for the occasion. The civilian leaders and the barrack commanders attended this gathering, which served its purpose of building a good relationship between the captives and their captors. After dinner, Mr. Shaukat's daughter Saeeda tied a Rakhee (bracelet) around the wrist of Captain Jarreth. This is a popular annual tradition in India in which sisters tie a Rakhee on their brother's wrist, symbolically protecting them and wishing them success. Captain Jarreth was kind enough to complete the ritual and brought in gifts for Saeeda a few days later.

Toward the end of our captivity, Harnam Singh found another way to keep us occupied.

"I will show you a Bollywood 'fillum' every fortnight," he said as he puffed up his chest during one of the morning fall-ins.

Every other Tuesday, an Indian Hindi movie was shown. It was quite an event for which the prisoners would eagerly wait. The name of the upcoming movie would be revealed a couple of days before the screening, thereby increasing everyone's excitement and anticipation.

Early in the afternoon, Shastri would escort a white minivan into our cage, and they would install a reel movie projector. A big, white, theater-like cloth screen would be erected at one corner of the northern field. Horn loudspeakers were used for the sound system. Both the quality of sound and picture were poor, but we still loved watching the movies. By late afternoon, families would start laying down bedsheets or some other piece of linen to claim their territory in the grassy field in front of the screen. The movies would start after dark and usually last for two to three hours. At least for that long, the prisoners would forget their miseries and escape into a make-believe world.

I remember we watched some famous movies such as *Pakeezah* (1972), *Anand* (1971), *Mughal-e-Azam* (1960), and *Chaudhvin ka Chand* (1960), and we thoroughly enjoyed them.

Almost a year had passed by, and we were still in Camp #34 in Roorkee. We slept, ate, prayed, and played. We followed the same routine every day. Not much had changed.

20
The Long Days

As days passed, we settled into a dreary routine. We ate three times a day, prayed in the mosque, played in the fields, and went to Quran classes. The adults completed the numerous chores Harnam Singh had assigned them. They cooked, cleaned the grounds, swept the barracks, painted the walls, and kept themselves busy.

Nevertheless, the months of captivity were taking a toll on the minds and souls of the prisoners. The barbed wire cages were a constant reminder of their captive state, and with no end in sight, many slipped into depression and despair. Many women, as well as men in my barrack, were visibly withdrawn; they did not talk to anyone and just spent their entire day in the small floor space that was their home. There were no psychiatric medications or counseling available, and often, their only recourse was prayer and their firm belief in God, which kept some of them going.

As time passed, we spent more and more time in prayers and supplications. We recited many prayers from the Quran. In particular, the supplication of Prophet Younus while he was a captive inside the whale became very dear to the prisoners, and they would recite this prayer over and over again. "Our Lord! We have sinned against ourselves and unless You grant us forgiveness and bestow Your mercy upon us, we shall most certainly be lost."

The Quran said when Prophet Younus was thrown into the water and scooped up by the enormous jaws of a whale, he repented to God and repeated the above supplication often. Prophet Younus lived inside the bowels of the whale, and after three days and three nights, God listened to his prayers, and the fish spat him on the shore. But we had been reciting this prayer for more than a year, and God was yet to listen to our prayers. The story of Prophet

Younus taught us to be patient in the face of adversity, and we resigned to His will.

For children like me, life wasn't too bad, but for my parents and the other grownups in Camp #34, these were hard times. They put on a brave face and stood strong as best as they could, but I can only imagine how my parents must have felt to live on a six-by-eight piece of hard cement floor when, not long ago, they had lived in opulence in a big house, surrounded by servants. Though Ammi and Pappa both put up a brave face for us, I am sure now that this was the lowest point of their lives and that they kept going for our sake.

Ammi was the bedrock of our family and our source of strength. She was so brave she could even stand up to Harnam Singh. With her around, I wasn't afraid of the big, gun-toting Indian soldiers. Even when she was stressed, she would clench her jaw and press her lips together into a wide smile. I never saw her scared or afraid.

Ammi spent most of her day in the six-by-eight-foot area that was our 'home'. She would wake up early in the morning for Fajr prayers and then would clean up our little space of floor to prepare for breakfast. After breakfast, she would clean our 'home' again and pray again.

She not only offered the five daily prayers but also offered many non-obligatory prayers throughout the day and night. For hours, she would recite prayers on the beads of her rosary. She had a brown, leather-bound Quran that she had carried with her from Dacca, and she read it for hours each day. She had received this Quran as part of her dowry on her wedding from my grandparents. This Quran was one of the few possessions she took when my family fled our home in Narayanganj. It was her prized possession, and she kept it in immaculate condition, wrapped in a clean cloth envelope inside the metal suitcase.

As our captivity lengthened, her inclination toward religion increased, and she spent more and more time praying for our release.

We solemnly observed the first anniversary of the fall of our beloved Dacca on 16 December 1972. The atmosphere was very somber and gloomy. We'd been imprisoned for a whole year, and there was no hope of release in sight. Those were our low days.

As the imprisonment dragged on, many started losing hope. The trauma and stress of the horrors they had experienced in the aftermath of the 1971 war took a heavy toll. Almost everyone suffered from post-traumatic stress disorder, and while some found comfort in prayers and supplications, others were visibly depressed. And there were no resources to care for those who 'went crazy' during the 23-month ordeal. The MI Clinic had no psychiatric facilities or medications, which meant these mentally ill prisoners lived in the barracks along with all the other prisoners. Their poor families had a further traumatic time caring for these unfortunate patients.

For most captives, faith in God was what kept them going. Prayers were held five times a day in the camp mosque, and people spent hours praying and offering supplications. Their conviction that God would never abandon them was their source of strength, and they prayed for deliverance. They recited Ayatul Kursi and Durood Shareef day in and day out, and many stayed in the mosque late into the night to continue to offer prayers.

Many prisoners found consolation in the fact that our beloved Prophet Mohammed PBUH himself had migrated from Mecca to Medina in 622 CE to escape persecution. So, our Prophet was once a refugee himself, and just like us, he had to leave his home under adverse circumstances. In Islam, anyone who is forced to leave their home under the threat of oppression is considered to be walking in the shoes of Prophet Mohammed PBUH and, hence, held in high esteem. God himself proclaims in the Quran that people who migrate will have a higher status on the Day of Judgement and are considered honorable in His eyes.

"As for those who emigrated for the sake of God after having been persecuted, we will provide them with a fine abode in this life; yet better still is the reward of the life to come."

At least, God's promise made us happy that our hardships are not in vain and we will be rewarded for our sufferings in the hereafter.

We observed the Holy Nights, including Shab-e-Meraj, Shab-e-Barat, and Laylatul Qadr, and we prayed with great enthusiasm and reverence. During those special nights, I prayed with my parents. Most adults stayed up all night praying for our release. Eid Milad-un-Nabi, the anniversary of the Prophet's birth, was also celebrated with great devotion. We would hold special gatherings, and even we children participated in the prayers. The kitchen volunteers would prepare sooji ka halwa or other sweets for these auspicious occasions.

Shab-e-Barat or the Night of Salvation was celebrated with special fervor. It is said that God decides every soul's fate for the upcoming year during this night. Anyone who spends the night in prayers will receive deliverance. So, we stayed up late through the night into the early hours of the morning praying for forgiveness and for our release from prison.

During Ramadan, we fasted from dawn till dusk. We observed the Holy Month twice during captivity, once in November 1972 and again in October 1973. During Ramadan, we prayed even more and begged the Almighty for our release. The langar volunteers prepared and served food before dawn and again after sundown, and I remember getting roti with gravy for the early morning meal. For the evening Iftar, we would get dried dates along with either boiled chana daal or kala chana.

Though I was very young and not required to fast, I remember waking up at around four in the morning to eat with my family. We would sit cross-legged on the floor of our corner of the big hall and eat from a common bowl.

Although we knew there were four POW camps in Roorkee, we did not have a clear view of the other cages. Really, the only surroundings we could see during these two years were the barbed wire fences and the Himalayan Mountains far away beyond the north side fence, and after a while, the scene became quite monotonous and uninteresting.

Harnam Singh did his best to keep everyone occupied, but with men being men, some did get into trouble. There was the occasional heated argument over a petty issue. Sometimes, though rarely, men would get into fistfights, usually because someone jumped the line at the water tap. These incidents were dealt with sternly. The perpetrators would be assigned 'fatigue' or sent to solitary confinement.

Women had their fair share of altercations as well, and again, most often these were due to someone jumping the line at the ladies' shower. Some women would place small colored ribbon threads on a rope to mark their position in the shower line, and invariably, someone would jump the line, and an argument would ensue.

At the same time, some of the men created a different kind of squabble. These were men of the wealthy Chinioti families who owned tanneries and furniture industries in East Pakistan. They felt they were special and demanded better treatment than others, less fatigue duties, more food, and first dibs in selection of warm clothing that were occasionally distributed by the Indian Army. Even during the imprisonment, they had a more privileged lifestyle, thanks to the extra money they had somehow managed to smuggle into the camps by bribing the Indian Army guards. Mr. Quddus and the elders of the camp helped tame them down.

In summer, there would be long queues in front of the water tap in the center of the cage. Summers in Roorkee were long and hot, and because there weren't many trees, the only shade was under the asbestos-covered veranda, which got pretty hot too. We had some flask-shaped Surahis that we used to fill up at the water tap, and these earthenware clay pots would keep the water cold, even during the heat of the day. We had some stainless-steel drinking glasses, too, and I remember that when we poured cold water from the Surahis into the stainless-steel glasses, they felt very nice and chilled. We would also dampen the hanging bedsheet around our living space to make our little 'home' cooler. The barracks had no ceiling fans, but we were able to buy some handheld fans from the Military Commissary store. Sometimes, we would wet these paddled straw fans to provide a cooling effect.

Winters were not freezing cold, but without proper clothing and insulation, we shivered throughout the night. Most of us didn't have sweaters or wool clothing, nor did we have thick mattresses to cover the cold cement floor. Sleeping on the cold floor was very uncomfortable. The old brick walls didn't provide much insulation, and most of the windows did not close properly. The guards wouldn't let us close the doors due to security concerns, so it would get really chilly inside the barracks rooms. At night, we would huddle around our makeshift stoves for warmth.

Electrical power outages were also quite common, and the nights were often pitch dark. We had bought some wax candles and kerosene hurricane lamps from the Military Canteen store. These hurricane lamps also came in handy for walking between barracks during dark nights.

In the evenings, men would gather on the veranda to play card games or talk. We would sit in a circle and intently listen to our transistor radios. We longed to hear some news about us, the Pakistani prisoners of war in the Indian camps. But night after night, there was none. It really did seem as though the whole outside world had forgotten about us. There was no news about the 93,000 prisoners of war on the airwaves. We felt very lonely and isolated.

21
Terrible Times

These were some tough times. Month after month, we had no news of our fate. We were in limbo.

The living conditions for the prisoners inside our barracks were pretty bad. The old barracks had been erected in 1854 and had not been well maintained. The gray cement floor was chipped in many places, exposing the concrete slab underneath. There were cracks in the walls, and the hinged windows did not close fully. Cockroaches, rats, and rodents ran around both outside and inside the living quarters, where we were eating and sleeping.

More problematic were the head lice. They were highly contagious, and nearly everyone in the camp suffered from painful bites to their scalp. We had no medication for head lice, and my mother bought double-sided and fine-toothed nit combs from the Military Canteen store to remove the lice from our hair. Bedbugs were also rampant, and we frequently suffered from itchy welts all over our body. Some of us also suffered from scabies, and I remember the cracks in the skin between my fingers were very painful.

Seasonal illnesses, such as the flu and the common cold, afflicted the residents commonly. The lack of proper winter clothing, along with malnutrition, immune suppression, and improper living conditions, contributed to diseases. Flies and mosquitoes were more than a nuisance; many people in the camp contracted malaria from mosquito bites and had to take quinine. Hygiene conditions were not very good, and that led to outbreaks of dysentery and other waterborne illnesses.

We slept on the hard, cold cement floor – no mattresses, only our bistar bund to provide some cushion. Our small enclosure was marked on the sides with our meager belongings. Ammi slept by the wall, Pappa slept on the other side of our space, and three of us slept in between them within the six-by-eight-foot space.

Food was served three times a day, but if someone missed the food distribution time for their barrack, they would go hungry. Furthermore, the food we did receive was not always adequate in quantity. Civilian prisoners were provided only with sustenance rations. Each person would receive a small amount of rice or one roti, along with a little bit of the day's curry, which was usually too thin. We would often eat the rice or roti with South Asian pickles. We frequently went to the kitchen to gather roti pieces that were being thrown away, which Ammi would dry and store. Later, she would use them to make tortilla soup. She would boil the roti pieces in water and just add salt. It was a simple recipe but very filling.

Rice and daal were the staple foods during these two years. Daal was served so frequently that soon everyone became sick of it. We would often find little brown insects in the grain. The brown-black weevils would stand out among the white rice, and we would have to pick them out before eating. I remember plucking off weevils from the cooked roti before consuming it. The Indians would not allow the kitchen volunteers to wash or clean the grains because they feared that precious food grains would be lost during cleaning. So, it was quite common to bite into small concretions or pieces of gravel when eating.

Many captives suffered from malnutrition due to inadequate food and a lack of essential nutrients and vitamins. We suffered from chapped lips due to excessive sun exposure and lack of vitamins, as well as cracked feet due to poorly fitting shoes or walking barefoot. Many people experienced weakness and fatigue due to anemia from a lack of iron in a diet that was lacking in meat. Joint aches and muscle pains were common due to a lack of vitamins.

Perhaps the group that suffered most were the infants and young babies. Children under the age of one were provided 500 ml. of milk per day, and those over the age of one were given 250 ml. plus one roti. The milk provided was insufficient for the nutrition of the growing body, and these babies were too young to chew rotis. Many parents resorted to buying powdered milk from Bania, who quickly raised the price.

Many prisoners felt they were just living in a nightmare, and soon they would wake up and everything would be fine. Many could not reconcile themselves with the fact that Dacca was lost forever.

Every family in Cage #1, Camp #34 had a story to tell. They had lost everything that they had in East Pakistan. They had lost their properties, their businesses, and their jobs. Some had paid even more dearly with the lives of their loved ones. Many prisoners had a family member who had been killed, maimed, or raped by the Mukti Bahini.

Pappa was a heartbroken man. He had given his entire youth to the Adamjee Group of Companies, and now he had lost his job, his retirement plan, and his pension. He had lost his savings, his house, and everything he had built for himself. He would lament how the mill workers and laborers had turned against him just because he was a Bihari. Even his Bengali friends had turned their backs on him, and they changed from being friends to foes within a matter of nine months. He used to say, "When you are in trouble, no one is your friend."

He often mused over some verses from a poem that was famous in those days.

Ae Mere Humnasheen Chal, Kaheen Aur Chal
Iss Chaman Mein Abb Apna Guzaara Nahin
Baat Hoti Gulon Takk To Seh Letay Hum
Abb To Kaanton Pay Bhi Haq Hamaara Nahin

O' my beloved, go, let us go somewhere else.
There is no place for us in this Garden of Eden.
If it was only for flowers, I would have endured.
Not even the thorns belong to us anymore.

Gulsitaan Ko Lahoo Kee Zaroorat Paree
Sabb Se Pehli Hee Gurdann Humaari Kattee
Phir Bhi Kehtay Hein Mujh Se Yeh Ahl-e-chaman
Yeh Chaman Hai Hamaara, Tumhara Nahin

When the flowerbeds needed blood,
My head was first on the gallows.
And yet, people of this garden say,
Ours is the garden, not yours.

All the inhabitants in Camp #34 were refugees who had escaped with barely the clothes on their backs and a few precious belongings. As the months passed by, wear and tear became an issue, and proper clothing was a big problem. The Military Canteen store did not sell clothes. So, the only way we could get new clothes was if our relatives sent us some. But many people received no parcels during those two years, so the prisoners mostly wore old, worn-out clothing that had been repaired multiple times. My mother had a sewing kit, so she would mend and patch our shirts and pants frequently. I had a green sweater that kept developing big holes, and my mother patched it many times. I was lucky, too, that I inherited my older brother's clothing once he outgrew them. My brother faced more of a challenge, but many families in the camp swapped their children's clothing with their friends and neighbors as the kids continued to grow.

During the winter, the lack of warm clothing was a problem. The older prisoners suffered the most, and some had to be admitted to the Military Hospital with pneumonia. In Dacca, the Red Cross had given us some woolen blankets, and we also received some khaki-colored winter military-style sweaters from the Pakistan Army warehouse. On a couple of occasions, the camp administrators supplied us with thin woolen blankets or shawls. Many prisoners used to wrap themselves with them like a cloak to stay warm.

Though every season and every month was tedious and dreary, Muharram, the first month of the Muslim calendar, was particularly hard on the prisoners. It was during this month that in 680 AD, family members of the Holy Prophet Mohammed PBUH (Peace be upon him) were uprooted from their homes in Medina and took refuge in Karbala, Iraq. Here, the Prophet's grandson, Hussein, and his companions were mercilessly killed for refusing to pledge allegiance to an unjust king. The woman and children were rounded up, chained, and taken as prisoners 500 miles away to Damascus. The Battle of Karbala has been remembered by Muslims for centuries as the struggle against oppression and tyranny. We commemorated the martyrdom of Hussein during the first ten days of Muharram and grieved for the members of the Prophet's family. Many found poignant parallels between their story and our situation.

The prisoners felt very confined within the cages. They lived by a set of rules imposed by the Indian military, and these rules were strictly enforced. Anyone breaking the rules would be assigned 'fatigue', which meant they would be taken out of the camp and assigned laborious tasks in the woods. The forced labor would continue for several hours nonstop, under the watchful eyes of armed soldiers. Sometimes, the camp would be punished for the bad behavior of a few. All the male prisoners would be made to stand for an hour or so in the sun during the daily morning roll call.

Other forms of punishment included solitary confinement in a dark room behind the langar, which, after a couple of days, became very traumatic. When people came out of the dark room, they were extremely disoriented and would not be able to open their eyes. Hands-up punishment was yet another dreaded form of punishment. For this, the prisoners were made to raise their hands above their heads in a stress position and would remain this way for thirty to forty-five minutes in the blazing sun. An Indian soldier would stand in front of the culprit with his .303 rifle pointed. The hands-up position becomes very painful within ten or fifteen minutes, and most people were crying by the end of their ordeal, but they didn't dare to lower their hands.

As I've said before, we were not allowed to go near the barbed fence. Anyone who came within a yard of the fence was punished. They would have to stand for over half an hour at that very spot with their hands raised up. The soldier would stand on the opposite side of the fence with his rifle pointed at the prisoner, ensuring that the hands would not come down, even momentarily. Once, my brother accidentally touched the fence while trying to retrieve a ball from under the barbed wire. The sentry, on the other side of the barbed wire fence, saw the infraction and immediately took aim and ordered my brother to stand in the blazing sun with his arms extended skyward. Some people in the camp saw the incident and quickly reported it to my father, who ran to the fence. When Pappa arrived at the scene, Khusro Bhaijan was standing with his hands up, trembling, and facing the sun. The guard's .303 rifle was aimed straight at Khusro Bhaijan's chest, his fingers on the trigger, and the sun glistened from the surface of his bayonet. Pappa gently persuaded the guard to let him go. It took quite a bit of doing, but the sentry knew my father was the barrack commander, so perhaps that was why he was lenient with my brother.

My brother was lucky, as he was only thirteen years old at the time. In a similar incident, a civilian man in his thirties was shot in cold blood in broad daylight by an Indian guard. He'd been talking across the fence to a Havildar of the Pakistan Army in Camp #33 at an area where the corridor between the two cages narrowed to a small gully. He had just received a letter from his wife and jubilantly wanted to inform his Havildar friend about his family. In his enthusiasm, the man unconsciously touched the barbed wires. An Indian soldier noticed. In a second, he was on the scene yelling at the Pakistani prisoner for flagrant violation of the orders. The poor man probably complained, or maybe he said something because the infuriated Indian soldier shot the young man point blank. He died within minutes. Later, we were told that another soldier had planted a hunting knife next to the dead body to cover up the whole incident. The soldiers reported to the authorities that a prisoner had tried to escape by cutting the wire and, therefore, he'd been shot dead.

According to another version of the story, the young prisoner had sold an imitation watch or fake jewelry to the Indian soldier in return for cash, and that's how the altercation began. In any case, we later heard that the Indian soldier was eventually court-martialed.

There were many other such incidents in which prisoners appeared to have been shot at close range with or without provocation. In October 1972 alone, the International Committee of the Red Cross reported that at least fifteen Pakistani soldiers had been killed and more than twenty wounded by Indian guards in POW camps. Some of these killings appeared to be cold-blooded murder. In other incidents, the Indians acted in retaliation when Pakistani soldiers behaved defiantly.

More than a year into captivity, the prisoners were becoming more and more restive, and tensions were rising inside POW camps all across India.

These, truly, were some terrible times.

22
The World Outside Camp #34

Our contact with the outside world was minimal, at best. We had no newspapers, phones, or television, and we felt very isolated. The few radios in the camp and the POW Mail were the only sources of news for us. The postal service was inadequate, and in those days, mail usually took weeks. We were provided with India Airmail envelopes, and we would write to our families in Pakistan or India. Then, we would drop off our envelopes at the officers' mess and patiently wait for a letter in return.

Mail would come on Friday morning. The prisoners would gather in front of the officers' mess, hoping to hear their names called and to receive news of loved ones. Later, we started receiving some parcels from our relatives. These parcels would first be opened by a sentry and checked before being handed over to us. Mostly, the parcels would contain nonperishable food items such as South Asian pickles, sweets, beef jerky, or else personal care items and, sometimes, even clothes. Friday became a very special day for the captives, and many in the camp eagerly waited for the mail to hear news of their loved ones.

My family was lucky that Ammi's parents, who lived in India, wrote regularly and sent us parcels. In doing so, they kept our spirits up during these trying times. I remember receiving many letters of consolation and encouragement from my aunts and uncles. In fact, at one time, we were receiving so many letters and gifts that we became the envy of the camp. Someone nicknamed my father 'Mr. Parcelman'. The Indian military personnel also took note of this, and occasionally, during inspection, they would take some of our gifts and give them to others in more need. Of course, they told us about this, and we thought it was a kind gesture. Once, Harnam

Singh even asked my mother if she could spare one of her dresses for a poor woman who had lost her husband in the war, and my mother happily obliged.

A few prisoners in the camp never received any letters or parcels. They had not been able to establish contact with their loved ones in the outside world at all. One could only imagine what their families in Pakistan went through, no doubt believing their loved ones were either dead or missing in action.

On the other hand, these prisoners themselves were not sure of their family's fate back in Pakistan. They spent long and agonizing months alone with no news from their families.

For them, the only contact with the outside world were the few radio transistors in the camp. In the evenings, men would gather on the veranda and listen to their radios. The reception wasn't great, and we would spend a lot of time fixing and positioning the retractable antennas, trying to pick transmissions. There was a lot of static, but we could at least hear something about the rest of the world. We mostly listened to Voice of America and BBC Radio. *Sairbeen*, aired by BBC Radio Urdu Service, which was a popular radio program in those days, was our window to the outside world.

Later on, we started catching Radio Pakistan as well. In April 1972, Radio Pakistan started broadcasting live messages from the relatives of POWs in Pakistan. They would record these messages and broadcast them over the airwaves multiple times. It was a treat for the prisoners to hear their family members in Pakistan deliver short messages on the air. The three-to-five-minute messages were mostly words of encouragement, prayers for release, or birthday wishes. Sometimes, a family would announce a birth or a wedding in the family, and sometimes they would just say a short 'I love you' message. Many people in our camp received radio messages from their families, but we didn't have any close relatives living in West Pakistan at the time.

A few months later, Radio Pakistan also broadcasted the names of POWs in Indian camps. A list was compiled by the International Red Cross that contained the names and locations of both military and civilian POWs. It was a source of great relief for both the prisoners and their relatives in Pakistan to know about the whereabouts of their loved ones. Many prisoners as well as families back home found out about their relatives for the first time through these broadcasts. During one such broadcast, Pappa heard the name of his cousin, whom we had last seen in Adamjee Nagar. Apparently, the whole family was imprisoned in a camp in Meerut, a hundred miles south of where we were. Pappa was very happy to hear they were alive and safe.

We heard on Radio Pakistan that a group of young Bihari men had reached West Pakistan from East Pakistan via the land route. For months, they had traveled on foot, hitchhiked, and mingled with locals to avoid detection and had finally been able to cross illegally at the western border. We could only imagine the hardships they endured, but we were glad that they'd been able to make it back to Pakistan.

Some Biharis escaped from Bangladesh into Nepal. The Pakistani and Nepalese governments had come to an agreement that anyone reaching Nepal would be given free transit to West Pakistan. Many desperate Bihari families headed that way in order to escape the mayhem in East Pakistan. The only problem was that they had to cross a narrow strip of Indian territory to get to Nepal. My 10-year-old friend Naeem Ahmed's family hired an illegal border crossing broker (Dalaal) and paid him all their savings. The dalaal took them to an uninhabited area of the border and disappeared, leaving them stranded in the jungle.

My 13-year-old friend Syed Ali's family also made the treacherous journey to the border town of Janakpur in Nepal. Here, they were stranded without money or food for three months while the embassy tried to repatriate them to West Pakistan. Young Syed Ali sold cigarettes in Ratna Park in Katmandu to provide food for his family.

We also heard on the radio about the plight of Biharis who had been left behind in refugee camps in Bangladesh. The Indian Army's main goal was to evacuate the Pakistani military personnel and their families. But there were more than a million civilian Biharis in East Pakistan, and a very large number of them missed out on the transfer out of Bangladesh. We learned that they lived in terrible conditions in the Bangladeshi refugee camps. We felt bad for these stranded Biharis but also thanked God that, at least we weren't stuck in the quagmire that was Bangladesh. My family was among the few thousand lucky civilians who had made it out of Bangladesh along with the Pakistan Army. Though we were still caged prisoners in a foreign land, at least, we had hope that we would one day be repatriated to Pakistan.

On Voice of America, we heard that President Nixon and his administration were heavily embroiled in the Watergate scandal. Pakistan was an American ally in those days, and Pappa used to say that America would use its influence to broker a deal for our release. After all, a hundred thousand prisoners in POW camps were a challenge to the free world, and we prayed that the world leaders would intervene on our behalf. But now, with the political turmoil in America, President Nixon was less likely to get involved in our plight. We were sad to hear this news and felt hopelessly stranded on the international scene.

Every Wednesday night was a special treat on our radio transistors. We impatiently waited for 8 p.m. to arrive so we could listen to the *Binaca Geetmala*, a top ten countdown of Indian film songs presented by Ameen Sayani from Radio Ceylon. Ameen Sayani was a famous radio show host and celebrity, and millions of people all around the world listened to his program in the seventies. His unique style of addressing his listeners and his melodious, bubbly voice made him an icon, and to this day, many TV and radio personalities in the Indian subcontinent try to imitate his distinct style. Every week, he would play the top ten Bollywood songs on the chart. We would gather around the radio transistors and listen to these popular songs. Some people, inspired by the songs, would start to sing, and others played tunes on the harmonica.

But, for the most part, our days were monotonous, mundane, and terribly empty. Apart from the mighty Himalayas rising up beyond the north fence, all we could see around us were the other barbed wire cages. It almost felt like the camps existed in a vacuum and there was nothing or no one around us. Apart from the occasional chance sighting of an airplane very high up in the sky or the shrill dying whistle of a train going to Dehradun heard during quiet nights, there was not much outside sensory input for the inmates.

We didn't even have a good view of the other cages from our camp. The seven cages at Roorkee were separated by a ten- to twenty-foot dirt corridor, which was lined with barbed wire fence on both sides, hampering visibility. Armed Indian soldiers patrolled between the cages with their big and mean Alsatian dogs. They carried .303 rifles with open-blade bayonets and ensured that the prisoners did not approach the fence. In addition, soldiers closely monitored life in the camps from their watchtowers in the four corners of the camp, twenty-four hours a day.

Cage #3 of Camp #33, across from our cage, was for the military prisoners of war. Through the barbed wire fence, we could sometimes spot the Pakistani soldiers in the distance, wearing loose gray cotton uniforms. A large POW insignia with a cross mark was painted in black ink on the backs of their shirts so that they could easily be identified in case they escaped. The camp housed both officers and jawans of the Pakistani military. Some of the soldiers had been stationed in East Pakistan with their families. The families had been brought in with the soldiers but were now held in adjoining civilian camps. The soldiers were only allowed a short monthly visit from their wives and children.

Though the officers of the Pakistan Army were provided slightly better accommodations than us, they were also more heavily scrutinized. They were watched and guarded very closely and were subjected to three to four roll calls per day. Sometimes, they were even lined up on the grounds as early as 4 a.m. During the two-year period of our captivity, there were many attempted escapes. Mostly, these came from Cage #3 of Camp #33, next door, that housed the military prisoners of war. These daredevil attempts were usually tried by the junior members of the Pakistani armed forces as the higher-ranking officers, such as majors and colonels, were either more mature or physically less capable of such daring acts. Most of these attempts were unsuccessful, but a few soldiers of the Pakistani Army did manage to escape by digging a tunnel. I'm not sure if they were later captured or not.

Most of the prisoners in our camp lived with their families, and so, the men from our cages were not inclined to escape. Still, a few civilian bachelors attempted to break out. They would wait for overcast, moonless nights or for nights covered in a thick blanket of fog, and so, hidden, they would climb the barbed wire fence and run. Their plan was to simply run as fast as they could and to disorient the dogs by throwing pepper powder, stolen from the kitchen, at their noses. These plans did not work, and most escapees were shot dead. The few who survived were put in solitary confinement, where they were kept in total darkness for two months and fed very little. We heard they were physically and psychologically tortured as well. When they returned, they had lost more than half their body weight.

Outside the confines of our camp, there was a substantial population of Muslims in the town of Roorkee. They seemed quite concerned about the plight of us imprisoned fellow Muslims. One such person was Haji Saheb, a prominent local Muslim businessman. No one knew what his name was, but everyone called him Haji Saheb because he had been to Mecca and performed the ritual of Hajj. He somehow connected with Colonel Harnam Singh and offered to send in much-needed supplies to the prisoners. He arranged for day-to-day items like milk, food, and medicines to be delivered to Bania, who in turn supplied those items to us. Bania kept a register in which he entered all the supplies that came from Haji Saheb and who they went to.

In most cases, Haji Saheb paid for the supplies himself and didn't ask a penny from the prisoners. In some cases, our relatives would send in money to Haji Saheb with special requests. Haji Saheb was a God-fearing man who kept a thorough record and painstakingly entered all the transactions in his ledger. He would deliver those items to Bania, who passed them on to us. My grandmother also sent some money to Haji Saheb every month, and he diligently sent us additional food supplies through Bania.

My youngest uncle, Dr. Mujahid Hussain Qureshy, who at the time was a medical student in Hyderabad, India, was so thrilled to learn that we were alive that in October 1972 he traveled 1,700 kilometers from Hyderabad Deccan to see us for ten minutes. With Harnam Singh's special permission, my family went to the entrance gate of our cage. It was early in the morning and still quite chilly. My uncle stood on one side of the double barbed wire fence while we stood on the other side about ten feet apart. We were not allowed to speak or gesture. But when my uncle saw my brother shivering in the cold, he impulsively took off his sweater, tied it up into a bundle, and threw it over the barbed wire fence at us. The guards immediately took notice, confiscated the sweater, and reprimanded him sternly. It was a joyous meeting but very short and icy. At least, he was able to go back and inform my grandparents that we were alive and that he had seen us with his own eyes.

A few months later, the Indian government allowed immediate family members to see the captives on the occasion of Eid. The visitors would need to take a train to Delhi and, from there, travel by bus to Roorkee. Once in Roorkee, they would have to get a rickshaw to the outskirts of the camps. Here, they would be taken to a meeting room and body searched. The lucky prisoners would, then, be escorted in from their camps and allowed to meet their family members under the watchful eyes of an armed guard.

So, my uncle brought my grandmother to see us for Eid in January 1973. This time, we met in a small room in the army administrative quarters outside Camp #34. This room was located in a barrack next to the Military Canteen Store, and my family was escorted there by armed guards. We hugged each other profusely and cried. The room had no furniture, so we sat on a rug on the cold cement floor. My uncle and grandmother brought us warm clothes, food, and sweets, and I was as excited to see my grandmother as I was to see the candies she had brought.

23
The News Everyone Was Waiting For

In the early days of our captivity, spirits soared high. Everyone knew we had started our journey and that we were on our way to Pakistan. But as months began to pass without any news about our release, hope began to dwindle. Spirits sank so low that some even ceased to aspire for freedom. The 'camp' became a way of life, and we settled into a dull and dreary routine.

After more than a year and a half with no news, we felt we were doomed to live in the camps forever.

In August of 1973, the foreign ministers of India, Pakistan, and Bangladesh met in New Delhi to discuss our fate. Almost a year earlier, the prime minister of Pakistan, Mr. Zulfiqar Ali Bhutto, and the Prime Minister of India, Mrs. Indira Gandhi, had met at Shimla and signed an agreement that set forth the guiding principles to which both countries would adhere while managing relations with one another. The Shimla Agreement ensured that both countries would settle their differences through peaceful means and bilateral talks, and it paved the way for the negotiations that would lead to our repatriation.

We had heard on the radio that the foreign minister of Pakistan at the time, Mr. Aziz Ahmed, was in New Delhi to negotiate a deal for the repatriation of the ninety-three thousand military and civilian prisoners of war. The foreign minister of Bangladesh, Mr. Kamal Hossein, and the Indian foreign minister, Mr. Swaran Singh, also took part in this tripartite meeting. We longed to hear some good news, but the atmosphere in our camp remained somber and even gloomy. The negotiations dragged on, and there was no end in sight.

The Pakistani government insisted that all the land captured by the Indian Army on the India-West Pakistan front should be returned. Bangladesh insisted that the Pakistani military personnel who had committed war crimes against Bengalis should be tried. They compiled a list of 195 Pakistanis in Indian custody and charged them with genocide and crimes against humanity. Initially, this list was kept a secret as the Bangladeshi government started gathering evidence against these army officers. Some of these accused Pakistanis were rumored to be interned with their families in Roorkee. These military personnel were housed in Cage # 3 of Camp 33, while their families lived with us civilians in other cages. I remember there was a lady in our barrack whose husband was believed to be among those 195 Pakistanis.

The Pakistani government, however, strongly opposed this idea and maintained that such an action to try these soldiers would be in defiance of the Geneva Convention. Pakistan contested that during the war, the Pakistan Army was defending their own territory, and if any atrocities were committed, the Pakistani government alone had the authority to try the perpetrators.

The Indian government insisted that the POWs had surrendered to the joint command of India and Bangladesh, and, therefore, any decision about their plight should be made with the mutual consent of both countries. India also insisted that Pakistan must recognize Bangladesh as an independent nation before any solution could be negotiated. But they later softened their stance and entered into negotiations with Pakistan. Initially, Bangladesh had declared that it would not take part in any negotiations until Pakistan recognized the new country as a sovereign nation, but due to international pressure, they, too, backed off and entered the dialogue at the secretariat level.

But the fact of the matter was that the POW internment had dragged on far longer than anyone had anticipated. By the fall of 1972, India was reeling under the financial and economic burden of caring for and protecting almost a hundred thousand POWs and wanted a quick solution. These POWs were no longer a bargaining tool; instead, they had become a liability.

Pressure was also mounting on the Pakistani government to bring a resolution to the POWs' ordeal. With 93,000 prisoners in India, a very large segment of the Pakistani population was directly or indirectly affected, and many people had either friends or family in the Indian POW camps. Furthermore, public attitudes were sympathetic toward the imprisoned troops, who had sacrificed greatly trying to prevent the breakup of their country. Pakistanis demanded the safe return of their loved ones, and all over the country, everyday people protested and marched in support of the POWs. It was clear to all that both the Indian and Pakistani governments were under a great deal of pressure to resolve the issue of the prisoners of war.

During the tripartite meeting in New Delhi in August 1973, we were glued to the evening radio, even more so than usual. Because the reception was so poor and we kept hearing so much static, some of the men decided to go to the officers' mess, where the Indian guards had a properly functioning radio. After a little bit of persuading, they took pity and let them listen to their radio. Night after night, the prisoners of Cage #1, Camp #34 would gather in front of the officers' mess and listen to Voice of America. Pappa and Khusro Bhaijan would go to the officers' mess every evening and bring us the latest news.

On the night of 28 August, there was something in the air. I was in my barrack room, and a lot of people were getting ready to go to the officer's mess.

"Can I go, too, Ammi?" I asked excitedly.

"It's too late for you to go out," Ammi said.

"All my friends are going," I protested.

"OK, but stay close to your father and brother, and don't be going anywhere close to the fence!"

Ammi brushed up my clothes and combed my hair, and I tagged along with Pappa and Khusro Bhaijan. I was beyond excited to be out among the grownups so late in the night. A large crowd had gathered outside the officers' mess. We saw the grownups were very apprehensive, and some were clearly jittery. As the grownups gathered around the wooden stairs of the officers' mess, the Indian guards turned up the radio louder.

When the Voice of America newscaster announced that an agreement had been signed and all parties had finally agreed to the repatriation of the POWs, the crowd erupted in rapturous applause. We jumped for joy. We were deliriously happy. The Delhi Agreement started the repatriation process of the 93,000 Pakistani prisoners of war and civilians interned in the POW camps in India.

Everyone was jubilant, and no one knew quite how to express their happiness. Some laughed, and some cried. They thought of the days when they'd been hopelessly stranded in Dacca. Fear of loss of life and honor hung over their heads, and they were running out of food and shelter. They thought of how the Indians had brought them to the relative security of Camp #34, where they had a roof over their heads and food to eat. Indeed, though the twenty-one months of their imprisonment had seemed to last an eternity, now, after almost two years of captivity and endless prayers, they were finally going to be free. It was just too good to be true. Somehow no one could come up with the right words to thank God Almighty. Silent tears were the only expression some could manage.

The next day dawned bright and sunny. For the 840 prisoners in Cage #1, Camp #34, this was not just the beginning of another day. This day marked the beginning of the end of their ordeal. On that day, they woke up well before the first sign of dawn and offered the Fajr prayers in the mosque and thanked God for his mercy.

As the day progressed, we eagerly waited for more information. The old colonel was not late in coming, and at his heels was his right-hand man, Captain Ahluwalia, dressed, as always, in his crisp military uniform. A crowd converged around them. The colonel smiled empathetically; he, too, may well have experienced similar days.

"Kicking me out of my job? Eh!" He smiled broadly as he peered down at the jubilant crowd that had gathered around him under the peepal tree.

"*Badhai ho! Badhai ho!*" he said as he congratulated the prisoners.

"I 'whant' to tell you know I have talked to headquarters, and they have confirmed the good news you have heard last night."

The crowd cheered, and people hugged each other like schoolchildren. We were ecstatic.

Harnam Singh put his hands on his hips and said, "At this time, I have no more details, but the headquarters will let us know as soon as they have more information."

After one year and nine months, we finally had something to cheer about. Within a month, the repatriation process had started. The first trains full of POWs left from the camps in Northern India near the end of September 1973. The repatriation was covered closely by Radio Pakistan, and every evening, we would gather around the radio in the officers' mess to hear the news.

Almost every day, a train carrying eight to nine hundred POWs left India for Pakistan. Often, the names of the released POWs would be announced on the radio. For military POWs, we would hear their names and their ranks. Sometimes, we would hear familiar names and were delighted to know of their release. In a few instances, we even heard names of people who we had assumed to be either dead or missing, and that created additional excitement among prisoners. It was exhilarating, and everyone anticipated that very soon they, too, would be leaving for Pakistan, and it would be their own names announced on the radio. The excitement was almost unbearable.

A few days later, Harnam Singh informed us that we would be one of the first civilian groups to be released from the POW camps. The date of our repatriation to Pakistan was set for 29 October 1973. Just twenty-five days ahead.

24
The Preparations

The next twenty-five days were hectic but still interminably slow. Preparations for our release took place from dawn till dusk. For Harnam Singh, these were the last few days of his unblemished military career, and he wanted to ride into retirement with a special flair, all his own. He made sure the prisoners would practice their departure from India as well as their arrival in Pakistan. During the morning roll calls, every prisoner was instructed to put on the dress he or she would wear on the day of crossing and then line up in the grounds for inspection. Those who wore shabby dresses or those with even a small spot or stain were reprimanded and ordered to wash or arrange a new outfit. Shoes were to be polished, and those who did not have proper footwear were ordered to buy new shoes from the Military Canteen store.

Once during rehearsal, a poor woman appeared in old and shabby clothes. Harnam Singh was looking down the inspection line when he suddenly turned around and asked of my sister, who was blindly trailing behind him, "How many saris does your mother have?"

"Oh! She has many," Maliha Apa answered proudly, making a wide gesture with her arms.

"Good," chuckled Harnam Singh. "Then tell Mrs. Parcelman she has to give Sadaqa (charitable giving) in Islam."

The problem was thus quickly solved.

Attention then turned to everyone's luggage. Every bag, basket, or bistar bund was ordered out into the field. Old and tattered belongings were thrown away, thereby drastically reducing the amount of luggage in the camp. Our wicker suitcase did not make the cut and was determined to be too old and beyond repair, so it was thrown out. Suitcases and trunks were repaired and painted. The luggage was scrubbed and washed until our worn belongings looked spotless.

During one of the morning fall-ins, Harnam Singh stood under the peepal tree and declared, "'Phirstly', you will clean your luggage until it is 'shinny', then you will paint them. Then, you will write your name on every piece."

Harnam Singh looked at Captain Ahluwalia, who was standing next to him as he nodded in agreement.

"All the POWs" – he paused for a moment – "will make a 'laine' and 'whalk' in a single file. I 'whant' everybody to be orderly and follow SOP."

"I 'whant' the Roorkee contingent to be the number one contingent of POWs crossing the border." He forcefully raised his index finger up and clenched his fist to make the #1 sign.

The next day, Captain Ahluwalia provided us with paint. All the suitcases in the camp were painted dark green, and the name of the head of the family was painted boldly on the luggage, along with the CUPC prisoner number. I had been teaching myself calligraphy by copying my uncle's wedding card, so I wrote my father's name on our luggage in bold white and beautiful letters. Our little black suitcase was no longer black; it was a little green suitcase. Our bistar bund, brown leather suitcase, and the small green metal suitcase were all ready for the grand journey ahead.

Yet Harnam Singh was far from satisfied. This time, everyone was instructed to wear their best dresses and to carry their luggage as they would on the day of the border crossing. They were ordered to walk before the inspecting eyes of Harnam Singh, Captain Ahluwalia, and Captain Jarreth. Regardless, none of the prisoners seemed to mind these formalities and eagerly participated in the practice sessions. They happily carried their bags and marched across a make-believe crossing in the northern field. Everyone was happy to finally be going home.

However, strangely, a small group of prisoners were somewhat apprehensive about their release. These were the Bihari Muslims, whose forefathers had immigrated to East Pakistan. For generations, their families had lived in East Pakistan, adopted the Bengali culture, and spoke the language. They had never been to West Pakistan and had no idea of the life, traditions, or culture there. Now, they were being sent home to a new 'motherland', a strange place they had never seen before. One could easily understand their apprehension about going to an alien place that was to be their new home. Our cage commander, Mr. Quddus, was one of these individuals. His ancestors had immigrated to Bengal from the Assam province of India almost a hundred years ago. Even my family was in a similar boat, but at least we had visited West Pakistan a few times, and we had some relatives there.

The prisoners of Camp #34 were then sent to the MI room for medical inspection before repatriation. They were organized into groups of twenties and thirties prisoners and marched to the MI room guarded in the front and rear by Indian soldiers. Mr. Shaukat's swagger was even more obvious than usual as he proudly marched everyone back and forth from the MI room. On their way back, the prisoners would stop at the Military Canteen store and buy shoes and other necessities for the big journey ahead.

My turn came on a cold early October morning. I lined up in a single file with my family behind the main gate next to the officers' mess. Mr. Shaukat marched down the line like an army general inspecting his troops.

"*Chalo chalo...jaldi karo!*" he said at the top of his voice. A chill went down my spine. It was one of those times when I was excited and not afraid to go to the MI room.

Mr. Shaukat puffed up his chest, adjusted the straps of his medicinal bag over his shoulder, and waved his hand above his head, instructing us to move forward, and off we went to the MI room.

The Indian government wanted to show the world that the POWs had been well taken care of during the two years of captivity and that they had been properly treated according to the rules of the Geneva Convention. Therefore, special efforts were made in the last few weeks to ensure that prisoners appeared to be in good condition for repatriation. We were even given extra food and milk in the days preceding our release.

For the most part, the Indians had followed the Geneva Convention and treated the POWs fairly during our two years of imprisonment. We were treated with respect and dignity, and there was no unnecessary pestering or harassment of the civilian prisoners in our camp. Women and children were kept safe, too, and the guards didn't intrude inside the camps or terrorize the prisoners. We had even heard reports of Indian Army personnel showing respect and saluting the imprisoned senior-ranking officers of the Pakistan Army. However, the Geneva Convention does call for the immediate repatriation of prisoners after the cessation of war, and this did not happen. But, overall, the attitude of our Indian captors was not hostile.

A week before our release, jewelry and other precious items that the Indians had taken into custody at the beginning of our captivity were returned. This took place in one corner of the officers' mess. Mr. Quddus sat on the head of the desk as the prisoners lined up to get their precious goods back. As each person received their possessions back, they checked them and signed against their names on the black leather-bound register.

With only a few days to go, the camp was brimming with activity. Every aspect of the transfer was thought through and planned for. Clothes were washed, and shoes were polished. Food for the long journey was prepared in the langar. People stayed up late into the night, packing, unpacking, and rearranging their meager belongings in their bags. In fact, there was so much brisk and frenzied activity that one night, while I was preparing to sleep on my mat, I told Ammi, "I am so tired from packing all day, I fear I won't be able to get up tomorrow."

The day finally arrived, bright and beautiful. Everyone was up early, and by 6:30 a.m., the prisoners were out of the barracks and in the large field. We placed our belongings in a long line in the north field and took our places according to our serial CUPC (Civilians Under Protective Custody) numbers. This accomplished, the prisoners eagerly waited for the military trucks that would take us to the train station. By 8:30 a.m., the lorries had arrived.

Now, the long and slow process of registration and counting began. The head of each family was called out, the members of his family were counted and verified, and their luggage was checked in. This process lasted almost two hours, and then, finally, we were lined up and boarded the twenty or so Tata military transportation trucks parked next to the main water tap in the center of our cage.

Soon, the convoy of military trucks, with army Jeeps at the front and rear, started rolling down the gravel road leading out of Camp #34. As the convoy slowly moved through the barricaded gate, the sentries at the gatepost waved us goodbye. The trucks drove through the multiple layers of barbed wire fences, and the prisoners took a last look at the caged compound that had been their home for two years. They gazed with repugnance at the old and dilapidated barracks, into which they had been stuffed like sardines, but now they began to feel the fresh air of freedom. They were joyful that after almost two years they were beginning their journey to freedom.

After a short ride, we arrived at the Roorkee Railway Station. The small station had been built solely for military purposes and consisted of little more than a station building and an ammunition godown. But today, the station on the outskirts of Roorkee hummed with activity as it witnessed its first-ever assembly of a large and jubilant yet orderly crowd. The usually deserted station overflowed with the refugees and their guards. To obtain relief from the blazing sun, we huddled together in the specially erected tents and eagerly ate our lunch. Abandoning all formalities, a smiling Harnam Singh also joined the refugees and ate a phulka with us.

A diesel train engine with a long row of red carriages was waiting for us. However, this time, there were no wooden planks covering the windows. We felt relieved. The prisoners were counted and recounted and then led onto the waiting train. We were seated in the compartments according to our CUPC number. My family of five sat together on one wooden bench.

Once we boarded the trains, we were counted again. Finally, the doors were sealed, and five armed guards took up position in each carriage. We knew it was just a formality; only a fool would have thought of escaping today. But we also knew that Harnam Singh was the one to always follow SOP.

All this accomplished, Colonel Harnam Singh and Captain Ahluwalia themselves boarded a special compartment in the middle of the train. It was 4:30 p.m. We sat patiently inside the carriage, waiting for the journey to start, but as time passed, we started to grow impatient, and even seconds felt interminable. Everyone was happy but very tense. It seemed an eternity before the old locomotive came to life, roared, and whistled, and then we heard a familiar but long-forgotten thud as a buffer struck the buffer of our carriage. The train jolted, and the prisoners let out a thunderous cheer. The sound came again and again, and it came faster and faster and faster.

Someone shouted, "It's moving! It's moving!"

Everyone started cheering and embracing each other. We were on our way to Pakistan.

Soon, night fell. The train picked up speed and headed westward. In each compartment, there was a huge degh, full of rice and potatoes that had been brought in at Roorkee. It had been prepared by our langar volunteers, and we were served dinner from it. We ate, then sat back and tried to rest.

It was quite difficult to sleep that night because of the intensity of our excitement. Most people were talking loudly and laughing. Some people recited the Quran while others sang. And Saleem played harmonica all night long.

Due to a lack of bench space, people took turns lying down and resting. Among the passengers were people who had known the luxury of cruise ships and jetliners; however, this was probably the most exciting and memorable journey they had ever undertaken.

The train raced through the dark of the night until, at the break of dawn, it halted on the Indian side of the border. The prisoners woke to a beautiful, crisp morning; parallel rays of sunlight were shining through the canopy of tall trees. We had arrived at the 'Zero Point' on the Line of Control of the Wagah Border between India and Pakistan.

25
Return

I looked out of the train window. The outside world was beautiful. The entire countryside was drenched in the soft glow of the early morning sun. There was still a thin curtain of morning fog, and the air was crisp and fresh. The train had halted right in the middle of the railroad track just inside India. Majestic deodar trees rose up on both sides of the track.

The Indian Army soldiers brought sooji, paratha, and hot chai for the POWs, and we had breakfast in our train compartment. After we finished, we were counted and led outside of our carriages, hauling our luggage with us.

The excitement among the prisoners was palpable. We were all emaciated and beaten down from two years of deprivation, but our spirits were soaring high, and one could see the smile bursting out of our cheeks. We had our best clothes on and carried our refurbished luggage. Some POWs had their Qurans in stitched cloth bags that they hung around their necks. For many, the Quran was their most valuable possession, and they carried it proudly.

A rugged path led from the middle of the train tracks to a clearing surrounded by huge trees and lined on one side by wooden benches. The prisoners were told to sit on the benches in the shade of trees while the formalities were completed. Beyond the trees, we could see the road leading to Pakistan. Freshly whitewashed stone markers lined both sides of the road. A simple rail fence and a tall wrought iron gate marked the Indian side of the border between India and Pakistan. Just beyond the gate, a wooden pole gate marked the Pakistani side of the border.

From here on, time passed painfully slowly. From across the wooden rail fence, we could see the preparations taking place on the Pakistani side of the border. People were working frantically to welcome us to Pakistan, and in the distance, we could hear the Pakistan Army brass band playing our national anthem. The excitement was unbearable. Pakistan was so near, yet so far!

Chacha proudly sat propped up on a bench with his big wall clock on his knees. Perhaps he had the only functioning timepiece among the prisoners. He pointed to his clock and triumphantly displayed the time. A group of onlookers gathered around him. He announced, "Fifteen minutes." A few minutes later, he shouted, "Ten minutes!" And then, "Five minutes!"

He didn't say anything further but held his clock close to his breast, slung his bag over his shoulder, lifted his small suitcase, and triumphantly walked toward the narrow path that led to the crossing post. He stopped at one of the stone markers just before the crossing and put his stuff down. He stepped on his suitcase, proudly standing tall, then looked back at the other prisoners and smiled gloriously.

Others quickly followed his lead, and soon hundreds of smiling faces picked up their belongings and formed a straight and orderly line behind Chacha. At this moment, Harnam Singh strode in with his entourage and stood in front of the crossing gate. He looked intently down the long and orderly line and quipped, "Chacha, are you trying to take command from me? Don't you forget, I am still in charge, and I can lock you up for another two years."

He burst into laughter, and with that, the whole crowd did the same.

There was a brief ceremony in which the flags of the two countries were raised and the national anthems played. The wooden pole gate was lifted. The Indian soldiers shook hands with the Pakistani military officials. The International Red Cross representative checked our papers and organized us into batches of twenty. Colonel Harnam Singh and Captain Ahluwalia shook hands with us, and we were officially allowed to walk across the 'Line of Control' and into Pakistani territory. I held my small and freshly painted green suitcase in my hand and proudly walked under the raised pole gate into Pakistan. It was a tumultuous feeling. Some of the prisoners were laughing hysterically. Some were crying, but these were tears of joy.

On the Pakistani side, cheerful, welcoming songs played for us on the loudspeakers. The songs praised the bravery of our soldiers and glorified the people of Pakistan. One particular song, I remember, went:

Aye watan ke sajeelay jawano, mere naghme tumhare liye hain.

O' the brave soldiers of my land, my songs are but for you!

We were led into a large, flat marquee tent, where we were given a hero's welcome. The multicolored, patterned tent was decorated with colorful buntings that hung from strings crisscrossing the length of the shamiana. Miniature Pakistani flags dangled above our heads. Young schoolgirls showered rose petals on us as we walked on the red carpet. The atmosphere was very festive and uplifting. The then-president of Pakistan, Mr. Fazal-e-Elahi Chaudhry, came to receive us and spoke briefly to the crowd.

It was Eid ul Fitr day on 29 October 1973. Muslims all over the world were celebrating the joyous feast that marks the end of the Holy Month of Ramadan. It was a 'double Eid' for us, for we were celebrating two joyous events together. We offered Eid prayers in a big, open, and grassy area. The jubilation of celebrating two Eids was overpowering, and the crowd was overwhelmed with emotion.

We were treated to a sumptuous lunch of biryani and kababs and then registered by Pakistani officials and given train tickets to our final destinations in Pakistan. At that time, my father's older brother, Mr. Khawaja Karimuddin, was posted with Pakistan Railways in Lahore, just a few miles from the Wagah border. He came to pick us up and brought us to his home.

26
After the End

After spending a week in Lahore, my family used the tickets provided by the Pakistani government to travel to the southern port city of Karachi. Here, we lived with some of our distant relatives for almost a year while my father desperately searched for a job. The Adamjee Company flatly refused to rehire him, stating that they had themselves suffered significant losses as a result of the war and they could not possibly reinstate everyone. Not only did Pappa lose his job but he also lost his pensions and years of gratuity bonus that he had accumulated in service of Adamjee Jute Mills. Pappa finally found a lower-level job in the marketing department of Valika Cotton Mills in Karachi in August 1974.

The repatriation of POWs continued into the latter part of 1973 and early 1974, and by February 1974, most of the prisoners were returned to Pakistan. The 195 named war criminals were separated from the other POWs and moved from various camps across India to the Agra Jail. Here, they were imprisoned in two camps and guarded even more closely than before as Bangladesh prepared to move forward with their trial.

Pakistan continued to refuse to recognize Bangladesh as an independent nation. The trial of the 195 Pakistanis was the main point of contention. Bangladesh continued to demand that the Pakistani perpetrators of genocide must be punished. Both countries refused to budge from their positions.

The convening of the Islamic Summit Conference in Lahore in February 1974 in Pakistan proved to be a serendipitous opportunity for the resolution of this stalemate. The heads of state of 36 Muslim countries were gathering in Lahore, Pakistan, for this highly publicized event, and Bangladesh, despite being a populous Muslim country, was not formally invited. Both countries were under strong pressure from friendly Muslim nations to resolve this issue before the summit, an event that was supposed to showcase solidarity and brotherhood among Muslim countries.

On 5 February 1974, the secretary general of the Islamic Secretariat, Mr. Hasan-ul-Tohmay, visited Dacca in an attempt to convince Sheikh Mujibur Rahman to attend the meeting. Mujibur Rahman, however, refused to participate until Pakistan formally recognized Bangladesh.

Just two days before the start of the summit, the foreign ministers of Islamic countries adopted a resolution to send a special mission to Dacca as a last-minute attempt to persuade Bangladesh to attend. The mission succeeded in convincing Mujibur Rahman to drop the trials of the 195 POWs in exchange for the recognition of Bangladesh. Pakistan recognized Bangladesh on 22 February, the inaugural day of the summit, and that same evening, Sheikh Mujibur Rahman flew into Lahore to take part in the Islamic Summit Conference.

Once the case against the 195 so-called war criminals was dropped, the repatriation of the remaining POWs resumed. The last batch of prisoners crossed the Wagah border in April 1974, bringing an end to this unfortunate chapter in the history of the subcontinent. In a symbolic gesture, the commander-in-chief of the army in East Pakistan, Lt. General A. A. K. Niazi, was the last prisoner to be handed over to the Pakistan authorities.

My family and I were fortunate to be among the 93,000 POWs repatriated to Pakistan, but a large number of Biharis still remained in Bangladesh. By some estimates, in 1972, almost 250,000 Biharis were stranded in 66 camps across Bangladesh, unable to translocate to Pakistan. These people were branded as traitors by the Bengalis and were not welcome in Bangladesh because they had sided with the Pakistan Army in favor of a united Pakistan. They were not granted citizenship or voting rights but were forced to live as stateless people in crowded refugee camps without even basic amenities. Over the years, they built makeshift dwellings, and the camp became a way of life for them.

Ironically, the Pakistani government felt no obligation to take these refugees since most of these people had originally immigrated to Bangladesh from the Bihar province of India and so had no physical ties to the land of West Pakistan. The Pakistani government repeatedly cited financial constraints and a lack of the resources needed to relocate such a large number of refugees as the reason for the status quo. Furthermore, Pakistan's internal fragmentation, political instability, military dictatorships, and successive changes in governments ensured there was no one to look out for these Biharis. Though some Pakistanis did feel morally obligated to absorb these Biharis into Pakistan, there was no strong group rooting for their cause.

Over the years, some humanitarian agencies attempted to move these stranded Biharis to Pakistan. In the 1970s and 1980s, the United Nations High Commission for Refugees resettled almost a hundred thousand Biharis in Pakistan. In the 1990s, the governments of Pakistan and Bangladesh agreed to resettle more refugees. Pakistan resumed repatriation with the financial support of the Muslim World League, a non-governmental organization. However, this resettlement process did not last long due to another change of government in Pakistan.

For several decades, successive governments in Bangladesh treated those Biharis who had opted for repatriation to Pakistan as refugees, not as citizens. They were deprived of all basic human rights, including education and the right to self-determination, and faced social exclusion and discrimination in every aspect of life. Finally, in 2008, in the landmark case of Mohammad Sadaqat Khan and others vs. Chief Election Commissioner, the Supreme Court of Bangladesh decided that Biharis are citizens of Bangladesh and have the right to vote. Soon thereafter, the government granted citizenship to the stranded Biharis.

After the court decision, the Pakistani government saw little need to continue the repatriation process, so, by now, it has come to a complete stop. But many of these camp dwellers were Pakistanis at heart, and despite being eligible for Bangladeshi citizenship, they still feel a sense of loyalty to Pakistan and continue to yearn to go to Pakistan one day. They chose to remain in these makeshift dwellings and maintain their Pakistani identity.

In recent years, the Biharis have been given national identity cards and voting rights in Bangladesh, but they still face discrimination in everyday life. They are easily identifiable because of their accent, fairer color, bigger build, and the temporary camp address on their ID cards. This prevents them from running businesses, obtaining government jobs, and admission to public schools. Hundreds of thousands still live in small and makeshift huts in dilapidated camps, without access to basic amenities of life, such as clean drinking water, education, or healthcare.

Forty-eight years later, the future of these camp residents is still gloomy and uncertain. Cut off from society, these stranded Biharis still live in overcrowded camps ridden with disease and poverty, and their living conditions have only deteriorated due to population growth. To this day, the plight of the stranded Biharis remains a challenge to the civilized world's conscience.

27
Epilogue

Pappa: Khawaja Qumaruddin

After repatriation, Pappa had a difficult time finding a job, and so our hardships continued. These were some tough financial times, but we were hardened by our two years in the camps, so we were resilient, and we survived. Finally, Pappa got an entry-level job in the Valika Woolen Mill in Karachi, and we lived hand to mouth for the next four years. In 1978, he got a break and went to Saudi Arabia as an expatriate worker. Here, he worked in the accounting department of the Saudi Royal Parsons Company until his retirement in 1990. Pappa immigrated to the United States in 1996 and lived with my brother. During a visit to Pakistan in 2000, he died suddenly of a massive heart attack. Pappa was a man whose life had been turned upside down due to circumstances entirely beyond his control. But, at least, at the end of his life, he had the satisfaction of knowing his children were doing well in their professional careers.

Ammi: Fatima Qureshy Qumaruddin

Ammi continued to make tortilla soup for the next year or two, and it still tasted wonderful. She was the daughter of a high-ranking civil servant in the princely state of Hyderabad Deccan and had known an abundance of opulence. So, these were especially trying times for her. But throughout the adversity we faced, she continued to encourage us to get a good education. Her main focus in life was to give her children the best education that she could provide. And she did. She immigrated to the United States with my father. She peacefully passed away in 2012, surrounded by loved ones.

My Brother: Khawaja Nizamuddin Khusro

My brother continued to excel in his studies and attained the highest honors in every test he took. He achieved the third position in Karachi in the matriculation examination and then the coveted first position in the Higher Secondary School Certificate examination. He was admitted to the NED University of Engineering and Technology, where he continued his excellent academic record, attaining first position in all four years of his undergraduate studies. He was awarded a scholarship to the University of California, Berkeley, and completed his master's in structural engineering with honors. He now works as a structural engineer in Chicago. His son, Rehan Nizamuddin, is training to be a radiologist, and his younger son, Imran Nizamuddin, is a medical student. His daughter, Huma Nizamuddin, is completing her bachelor's degree in pharmacy.

My Sister: Nafisa Tahera Maliha

My sister completed her master's in home economics from Rana Liaquat Ali Khan University in Karachi and now lives with her husband and family in Chicago. Her son, Saad Ahmed, has a master's degree in computer science and is working as a software development engineer at Amazon. Her daughter, Sobia Ahmed, received her master's in public health and is working as a medical information specialist.

Me: Khawaja Azimuddin

While I did not do too well in my studies initially, my mother's persistence and encouragement paid off, and I was accepted to the Dow Medical College, Karachi, in 1981. After finishing my MBBS, I left for Great Britain to train as a surgeon. I passed my Fellowship of the Royal Colleges of Edinburgh and England at an early age and, in 1995, decided to move to the United States to further pursue a career in surgery. After short stints in New York, Pennsylvania, and New Mexico, I settled in Houston, where I live with my wife, Sama, and our two children, Anam and Ahad. Anam is starting her residency training in ophthalmology, and Ahad is starting at medical school. I am a practicing colon and rectal surgeon and specialize in minimally invasive surgery. I was one of the first surgeons in the country to adopt robotic colon surgery. As a surgeon, I love working with my hands and naturally found a hobby in ceramic tile making. Surgery and ceramic tiles are my two passions in life, and I find it difficult to decide which one is my hobby and which one I love more.

Glossary

Abduls – A common name for Bengali househelps in East Pakistan
Akashvani – Voice from the heavens (name of All India Radio)
Ammi – Mother
Anarkali – A legendary slave girl immortalized by the tales of her love affair with Mughal Prince Salim
Apa – Sister
Ayatul Kursi – 'Verses of the Throne' from the Quran is believed to grant spiritual or physical protection
Badhai Ho – Congratulations
Bakra Eid – Muslim festival commemorating the sacrifice of Abraham (Eid ul Adha)
Balti – Bucket
Bangabondhu – Friend of Bengal
Bania – Member of an occupational community of merchants, moneylenders, shopkeeper
Banyan – A loose, T-shaped, one-piece upper body garment
Bara Khana – A military-style big feast for the entire unit
Begum – Lady
Bhaijan – Brother dear
Bhasha – Language
Bibi Ji – Ma'am
Bihari – People from the Bihar province of India, a general term used to identify all non-Bengalis
Bismillah – The ceremony marking the start of formal education of a child
Bistar Bund – Sleeping bag with pockets for storage of items
Chaat – Savory snack typically served as a hors d'oeuvre at roadside tracks from stalls or food carts
Chacha – Uncle

Chai – Milk tea
Chalo Jaldi Karo – Let's go…Hurry up!
Chapatti – Tortilla, flat, round bread made by slapping the dough between the wetted palms of the hands
Chappals – A pair of slippers
Chowkidar – Security guard
Chole – Spicy white chickpeas dish used as snacks
Daal – Lentil
Deghs – A big cooking pot
Dhoti – A garment worn by male Hindus, consisting of a piece of cloth tied around the waist and extending to cover most of the legs
Durood Shareef – Arabic phrase which contains salutations upon the Prophet of Islam
Eid – An occasion for celebration. Commonly used to denote the two festivals (Eid ul Adha and Eid ul Fitr) in the Muslim calendar
Eid Milad un-Nabi – Day marking the birth of the Prophet of Islam
Eid ul Adha – Muslim festival commemorating the sacrifice of Abraham
Eid ul Fitr – Muslim festival marking the end of the fast of Ramadan
Fajr – Early morning Muslim prayers
Fatiha – Prayer offered for the deceased
Ghee – Clarified butter
Haj – Annual pilgrimage to Mecca and commemorating the sacrifice of Abraham
Hajjam – Barber
Halal – Meat prepared in accordance with Islamic law
Arhar – Split red gram
Havildars – Rank in the Indian and Pakistani armies, equivalent to a sergeant
Iftar – Traditional breaking of fast at dusk during the month of Ramadan
Ishraq – Muslim mid-morning prayers
Jawan – Soldier, noncommissioned infantryman
Jalebi – Sweet made of a coil of batter fried and dipped in sugar syrup
Jumu'ah – Obligatory Muslim Friday congregational prayers
Kabaddi – A contact team sport originating from India
Kabooter – Pigeon
Kala Chana – Dark-colored chickpeas

Khatam-e-Quran – The ceremony marking the completion of the Quran recitation of a child

Kachoris – Round ball made of flour and dough stuffed with daal and chilies and deep fried

Kurta – A loose collarless shirt

Laylatul Qadr – Night of Decree or Night of Destiny is the night when the first verses of the Quran were revealed

Langar – Communal free kitchen

Lungi – Sarong-like long piece of cloth worn as a loincloth

Masoor – Split red lentil

Majhis – Boatmen

Moong – Split green gram

Mukti Bahini – The Bengali Militiathe

Namak Pare – Salted, deep-fried tortilla pieces

Nani – Grandmother

Nikah – Muslim marriage ceremony and exchange of vows

Nishan-e Jurrat Paan – The third highest military award of Pakistan

Palak – Spinach

Pan – A popular Southeast Asian snack made from betel leaf, chopped betel nut, and slaked lime

Pappa – Father

Pathan – A member of the Pashtun tribe hailing from the northern areas of Pakistan and Afghanistan

Phulka – Cooked, thin, flat bread

Pittu – Seven stones game

Puri – Deep-fried, soft, flat bread, sopapilla

Kameez – Long, loose shirt often worn over a shalwar

Qirat – Art of recitation of the Quran

Quran – Muslim Holy Book

Ramadan – The holy month of fasting. The ninth month of the Muslim calendar

Roti – flat bread

Sabzi – Vegetables

Sadaqa – Charity

Salan – Curry

Samosas – A triangular pastry case, filled with vegetables or meat and spices and fried

Sampan – A flat-bottomed wooden boat that often has a small shelter for permanent habitation
Saris – Female garment typically wrapped around the waist, with one end draped over the shoulder
Shab e Barat – Night of salvation, or the night when God decides the fates of people for the upcoming year
Shab e Meraj – Night of Ascension of the Prophet to the heavens to meet God
Shakar Pare – Sweetened, deep-fried tortilla pieces
Shalwar – A pair of light, loose, pleated trousers tapering to a tight fit around the ankles
Shamiana – A colorful decorative tent commonly used for outdoor parties
Sooji ka Halwa – A dessert made with semolina, milk, and sugar
Surahis – Clay pots with a long neck, used for storing and cooling water
Surahs – Chapters of the Quran
Talab – Pond
Tasbeeh – Muslim prayer beads (rosary)
Tawa – Flat griddle that is used to make chapatti
Urad – Split black gram

Reviews

Brilliantly written……..Just could not put the book down. Congratulations on an absolute masterpiece. Very well narrated of a very challenging time. A great service for the millions of refugees all over the world.

– M Shahid Quraishi. OBE, President Royal Society Medicine, UK.

Great book written in a non-traditional style from the viewpoint of an 8-year old. I could not put it down and read it cover to cover in one sitting.

– Arif Gafur. President of TCF-USA, a US based non-profit.

"Delightfully clear, factual, and effective, this account brings the author's experience and the aftermath of the Indo-Pakistani War of 1971 to light while offering a sobering reflection on the plight of refugees worldwide. The book comes off as beautifully balanced, factually well-informed, and appropriate for both the casual historian or a more academic reader."

– The Book Review Directory.

"The Boy Refugee is a touching yet empowering tale of a young boy who always kept his positive outlook, even when living in desolate conditions. The author narrates his family life and how each of them had a battle of their own. The language is very simple, and that made it even more impactful. This story of resilience is a must-read."

– Readers Favorite.

"In his moving new memoir, The Boy Refugee: A Memoir from a Long-Forgotten War, Dr. Azimuddin takes readers on a captivating and emotional journey as he recounts his family's experience as civilian prisoners of war." The Asia Society "A poignant first-hand account of life as a refugee and prisoner of war is told from the perspective of an eight-year-old boy. It's humbling and eye-opening to see how quickly a comfortable, carefree life can transform into chaos and fear. This is a timely story detailing the experiences of refugees."

– Traci DeSplinter, Attending Gynecologist. Houston Methodist Hospital.

"The Boy Refugee's experiences and emotions are conveyed very clearly in an easy-to-read and digestible book that one wants to finish in a single sitting."
 – Mohsin K, Attending Pulmonologist, St. Lukes Hospital Houston.

"Once I started to read, I wanted to finish it all in one sitting."

– Shajee J, Amazon Reviews